SWINGOUT

A Lindy Hop Swing Dancer Screenplay

Christopher C. Odom

CreateSpace

Scotts Valley, CA

In cooperation with

Odom Books

Nashville, TN

Published by

CreateSpace

100 Enterprise Way, Suite A200, Scotts Valley, CA 95066

In cooperation with

Odom Books

135 Sundown Drive, Nashville, TN 37013

ISBN-13: 9781434896285 (paperback)

ISBN-10: 1434896285 (paperback) 1. Fiction

This is an Odom Books book.

SWINGOUT

A Lindy Hop Swing Dancer Screenplay

Christopher C. Odom

Swingout

FADE IN:

INT. SAVOY BALLROOM — DAY

SUPERIMPOSE

"HARLEM, MAY 22, 1927."

THE FLETCHER HENDERSON ORCHESTRA

plays on the stage.

> CURTIS (V.O.)
> We just got news Charles Lindbergh had
> safely crossed the Atlantic Ocean
> landing in Paris-

ALEXANDER "ALEX" WASHINGTON,

A young wide-eyed dreamy African-American 13-year-old stands
amidst a crowd watching two African-American couples battle it
out on the dance floor.

> CURTIS (V.O.) (CONT'D)
> There were only two couples left in the
> 1st Annual Harvest Moon Swingout. They
> were me--

"CURTIS" MOORE & BIG MABEL (23-years-old) dance.

> ALEX
> You go, Curtis!

> CURTIS (V.O.) (CONT'D)
> With Big Mabel. And Fancy Feet with
> Priscilla--

"FANCY FEET" JEFFERSON & PRISCILLA JOHNSTON (33-years-old)
dance.

> CURTIS (V.O.) (CONT'D)
> Charleston was the rage back then, but
> people had started to do the Breakaway.
> And that's when it hit me.

BIG MABEL

bumps into

CURTIS

He Breaks Away without letting go, pulling

BIG MABEL

back into him.

> CURTIS
> That's it! Let's Swingout like that
> again.

They repeat the action several times while Freestyling.

Curtis and Big Mabel

win the contest by maddening applause.

Charles Buchanan,

42-years-old, owner of the Savoy, makes his way to the center of the stage.

> MR. BUCHANAN
> The judges have made their decision.
> The winners of the 1st Annual Harvest
> Moon Swingout are Curtis Moore and Big
> Mabel.

Curtis and Big Mabel are bombarded by the crowd and carried off on hands and shoulders.

EXT. SAVOY - DAY

The crowd carries CURTIS AND BIG MABEL outside of the Savoy.

> BIG MABEL
> I can't believe we beat Fancy Feet and
> Priscilla. All I wanted to do was
> dance.

> CURTIS
> I am the King of Swing.

INT. SAVOY BALLROOM - DAY

Fancy Feet sits on the edge of the dance floor with his hands over his head.

Priscilla caresses him affectionately.

Swingout

                          PRISCILLA
              Let's go home.

Priscilla puts her arm around Fancy Feet, helps him up, and
leads him to the door.

EXT. SAVOY BALLROOM - DAY

Curtis and Big Mabel sign autographs and pose for pictures.

A REPORTER pushes through the crowd towards Curtis.

                          REPORTER
              What was the step you were doing?

Fancy Feet and Priscilla

walk out of the ballroom and onto the sidewalk near Curtis and
Big Mabel.

Curtis

ponders for a moment. He sees a

newspaper

The headline reads:

"CHARLES LINDBERGH HOPS THE ATLANTIC."

                          CURTIS
              It was the Hop--the Lindy Hop.

                          REPORTER
              Where did you get that move?

Fancy Feet and Priscilla

stare into Curtis's mouth.

                          CURTIS
              I made it up all on my own.

Curtis makes EYE CONTACT with

Fancy Feet

                          FANCY FEET
              Mother Fucker. Curtis was only doing
              variations on my Breakaways.

He shakes his head.

>   FANCY FEET (CONT'D)
>   He used me like a blueprint.

>   PRISCILLA
>   Let's retire.

Fancy Feet and Priscilla

walk away.

>   CURTIS (V.O.)
>   And that's pretty much how Swing
>   dancing started.

GERALDINE WITHERSPOON,

a sexy 33-year-old blonde, appears in the crowd.

She makes EYE CONTACT with Curtis.

They exchange alluring smiles.

She seductively disappears into the crowd.

ALEX,

approaches Curtis.

>   ALEX
>   I want to learn to dance just like you.

>   CURTIS
>   I don't give lessons.

>   ALEX
>   I go to every dance contest and
>   performance you do.

>   BIG MABEL
>   Aren't you little Alex, Mother
>   Washington's boy?

>   ALEX
>   Yes, ma'am.

                         BIG MABEL
          I know her from church. A real God
          fearing women. When I was sick, she
          helped take care of my kids. I owe her
          one. We rehearse every afternoon down
          at the Savoy with Richard and Little
          Mabel.

                         CURTIS
          I don't let people watch me rehearse.

                         ALEX
          Please!

                         BIG MABEL
          He's just a kid. All he wants to do is
          dance.

                         ALEX
          I don't even know how to dance.

                         CURTIS
          No.

                         BIG MABEL
          Come by the Savoy after school. Be
          sure to tell Ms. Clarke Curtis said it
          was OK. Now run along.

Alex grabs Curtis's hand.

                         ALEX
          Thanks.

Alex

skips off through the crowd.

                         CURTIS
          Remind me to change your nickname from
          Big Mabel to Big Mouth.

EXT. SMALL'S RESTAURANT — DAY

Geraldine walks into Small's.

INT. SMALL'S RESTAURANT - DAY

Curtis and Big Mabel finish eating lunch.

MABEL,

a 20-year-old simple waitress, clears away a few dirty dishes.

> BIG MABEL
> Didn't the helpings used to be bigger
> here?

> CURTIS
> No, you just used to be smaller.

> BIG MABEL
> You were always three biscuits and two
> sausages tall. I guess little elves
> don't grow. Excuse me while I go to
> the little girls room.

Big Mabel leaves the table.

> CURTIS
> While you're there, be sure to ask
> someone where the moose's manger is.

Geraldine

grabs Mabel's attention.

Mabel comes back to the table and clears away the rest of the
dishes.

> CURTIS
> Mabel, could I pay for the check now,
> please?

> MABEL
> Already been paid for.

> CURTIS
> By whom?

> MABEL
> Some fancy White lady.

> CURTIS
> Where is she?

                    MABEL
                 (points at window)
        There.

EXT. SMALL'S RESTAURANT - DAY

Curtis runs out of the restaurant.

He stops Geraldine.

                    CURTIS
        Excuse me. Aren't you Geraldine
        Witherspoon the famous actress?

                    GERALDINE
        How about a drink?

Geraldine gently nudges her chest forward causing Curtis to
glance at her BREASTS.

                    CURTIS
        It's good to be the King.

EXT. SAVOY BALLROOM - DAY

ALEX runs down the sidewalk and through the front doors of the
Savoy.

INT. SAVOY BALLROOM - DAY

the lionel hampton orchestra

rehearses on stage.

Curtis & Big Mabel and RICHARD "CRAZY LEGS" JENKINS & LITTLE
SALLY (21-years-old), practice a routine.

                    CURTIS
        Richard, I have an idea for a new exit
        for Big Mabel and I.

                    BIG MABEL
        Another new move? I can barely
        remember the last move you came up
        with. Can't we just dance?

                    RICHARD
        I like it when we don't look the same.
        Show us your move?

             CURTIS
I promise this is the last one, and
then we'll just polish what we already
know.

             BIG MABEL
This is the last time.

             CURTIS
Since I'm so small, wouldn't it really
be funny if you carried me off stage.

             BIG MABEL
Oh, hell no.

             LITTLE SALLY
Let me try it with you, Curtis.

ALEX

walks into the ballroom and takes a seat next to the edge of
the dance floor.

             ALEX
I think it's a great idea.

             CURTIS
Kid, you can watch, but not talk.
                (to Big Mabel)
Try and pick me up.

Curtis

jumps into Big Mabel's arms.

             BIG MABEL
Get down! I can't hold you.

             ALEX
What about if you got on her back?

             BIG MABEL
You aren't supposed to be talking.

             RICHARD
I'd like to see it.

Curtis jumps on Big Mabel's back.

             BIG MABEL
Get off my back.

9.

                         CURTIS
               Do you have me?

Big Mabel throws Curtis into the floor.

                         BIG MABEL
               Don't ever do it again.

                         LITTLE SALLY
               Are you all right, Curtis?

                         BIG MABEL
               What about me, Little Sally?

                         CURTIS
               Legs are stronger than arms. I don't
               want to just sit on her back. I'll
               have to think up something more
               creative.

                         BIG MABEL
               I don't like this move.

                         CURTIS
               It was a good idea kid. Wait until you
               see what we do tomorrow.

CURTIS

pats Alex on the back.

                         CURTIS (V.O.)
               Now, that I look back, that day was
               probably the first sign Alex was
               different.

                                   DISSOLVE TO:

MONTAGE

INT. SAVOY BALLROOM - DAY - 1929

ALEX (15-years-old) watches Curtis and Big Mabel (25-years-old)
Lindy Hop. He makes suggestions.

                                   DISSOLVE TO:

INT. SAVOY BALLROOM - DAY - 1931

ALEX (17-years-old) watches Curtis and Big Mabel (27-years-old) switch partners with Richard and Little Sally (25-years-old).

Little Sally smiles and holds onto Curtis affectionately.

ALEX claps.

DISSOLVE TO:

INT. SAVOY BALLROOM - DAY - 1933

ALEX (19-years-old) clumsily Lindy Hops with Little Sally (27-years-old).

Curtis (29-years-old) and Richard (27-years-old) watch and jeer.

DISSOLVE TO:

INT. SAVOY BALLROOM - DAY - 1935

Curtis & Big Mabel (31-years-old) and Richard & Little Sally (29-years-old) complete a performance before a large crowd at the Savoy.

They travel BACKSTAGE

where ALEX (21-years-old) waits with towels and water.

DISSOLVE TO:

INT. SAVOY BALLROOM - NIGHT - 1937

ALEX, now 23-years-old, Lindy Hops with Big Mabel (33-years-old) amidst a crowded dance floor. He is good.

Curtis (33-years-old) Lindy Hops with Little Sally (31-years-old).

She is in bliss.

Richard (31-years-old) shakes his head.

END MONTAGE

EXT. SAVOY BALLROOM — DAY

LEONARD "LENNY" CLEVELAND,

a 45-year-old intimidating African-American male with a single
streak of white hair in his head, strolls into the Savoy.

INT. SAVOY BALLROOOM - DAY

As Lenny passes by the front office, the cashier,

MS. SIMMS,

a matronly 40-year-old African-American woman, stops him.

> LENNY
> Tell everybody I'm not here today.

> MS. CLARKE
> There's a gentleman downstairs who
> wants to speak with you. The name is
> Fillmore.

> LENNY
> You're helpful.

Lenny walks DOWNSTAIRS.

A well dressed Caucasian 37-year-old society man,

MR. FILLMORE,

sits at a table sipping on a cocktail.

Lenny offers his hand.

> LENNY
> I'm the Floor Manager here at the
> Savoy. What can I do for you?

> MR. FILLMORE
> I need a couple of Lindy Hoppers for a
> party in Manhattan Wednesday night.

> LENNY
> Sorry, I'm all booked.

                    MR. FILLMORE
          If I don't get any Lindy Hoppers, my
          fiancée will leave me.

UPSTAIRS IN THE BALLROOM

Curtis rehearses with Big Mabel, Richard, and Little Sally.

The erskine hawkins orchestra

rehearses on the stage.

BIG MABEL

trips through a Free Spin.

                    CURTIS
          Stop thinking about lunch and try it
          again.

                    BIG MABEL
          Why don't you climb down off of your
          Big beanstalk, Jack, and let me take a
          break?

                    RICHARD
          I think we could all use a break.

RICHARD AND LITTLE SALLY

leave the dance floor and take a seat.

                    CURTIS
          I've never lost a Harvest Moon Swingout
          and don't plan to.

                    BIG MABEL
          If I don't break, I will break.

                    CURTIS
          I didn't realize buffalo could be
          broken.

                    BIG MABEL
          I never knew munchkins could talk.

BIG MABEL

walks off of the dance floor and kicks off her shoes in a
booth.

                         CURTIS
              Please. They have health codes here.

LENNY

walks into the ballroom.

                         LENNY
              Curtis, can I have a minute of your
              time? It's business.

                         BIG MABEL
              No problem, we'll give you two plenty
              of time--

Curtis grabs a seat next to Big Mabel and grabs her arm.

                         CURTIS
              Anything you say to me you can say in
              front my people.

LENNY

folds his arms and stares silently at Curtis.

BIG MABEL

struggles and breaks free from Curtis's grasp.

She walks away.

RICHARD AND LITTLE SALLY

join her.

                         CURTIS
                      (to Lenny)
              No.
                      (to his Lindy Hoppers)
              You can come back now. We're finished.

                         LENNY
              Curtis, I'm giving you one last chance
              to reconsider merging your team with my
              team. I need a couple--

                         CURTIS
              How many ways are there to spell "N"
              "O", hell no?

                          LENNY
          Fine. Mark my words Curtis Moore
          Snowden. You'll regret the day you
          decided not to become one of Lenny's
          Lindy Hoppers.

                          CURTIS
          I'm feeling regretful right now.

LENNY

storms out of the ballroom dreaming of his day of glory.

EXT. SAVOY BALLROOM — NIGHT

MARQUEE

"Billie holiday & jimmie lunceford. last night of first round
trials for harvest moon Swingout."

Alex waits in line with his 19-year-old partner, FREDA
FITZGERALD, who is as pretty as she is feisty.

They are accompanied by another couple, RICHARD (21-years-old)
and MARGARET (19-years-old).

TICKET WINDOW

                          MS. CLARKE
          Hello, Alex. It will be 85 cents each,
          please.

                          RICHARD
          I thought it was 30 cents.

                          MS. CLARKE
          It's 30 cents before eight o'clock.

                          ALEX
                    (to Ms. Clarke)
          No problem. Where do we sign-up for
          the contest?

                          FREDA
          Do you really think we have a chance?

                          ALEX
          All of the better Lindy Hoppers, like
          Curtis, have already qualified in the
          previous rounds. Trust me.

Alex pays Ms. Clarke for everyone.

INT. SAVOY BALLROOM - NIGHT

A 22-year-old BILLIE HOLIDAY sings an upbeat song with her band
at the 140TH STREET STAGE.

                        ALEX
              This joint is jumping.

                        WILLY
              There's Colored people in here dancing
              with White folk.

                        ALEX
              The Savoy Ballroom is the only
              integrated place in the entire country.

                        WILLY
              You mean I get to dance with White
              women?

                        ALEX
              I want to say hello to Curtis.

                        FREDA
              Let's dance?

                        MARGARET
              Freda, come with me to the ladies room
              first.

                        WILLY
              Why does it always take two women to go
              to the bathroom?

FREDA

rolls her eyes at Willy as

MARGARET

leads her away by the hand.

                        ALEX
              When are you and Margaret going to get
              hitched?

                              WILLY
              I'm still young and playing the field.

INT. LADIES ROOM - NIGHT

MARGARET AND FREDA

fix their makeup in the mirror.

                                        INTERCUT TO:

MARGARET AND FREDA IN LADIES ROOM WITH ALEX AND WILLY IN
BALLROOM

                              FREDA
              What are you talking about? He's got
              your nose wide open.

                              WILLY
              What's up with you and Freda?

                              FREDA
              We just dance.

                              WILLY
              Washington, just dance? Right.

                              FREDA
              We just dance.

                              MARGARET
              You mean to tell me you ain't never--

                              ALEX
              Never.

                              WILLY
              Not even a little--

                              FREDA
              Just dance.

END INTERCUT SEQUENCE

                    WILLY
          Then you need to stop spending so much
          time together. How are you ever going
          to expand your horizons if you keep
          chasing sunsets?

                    ALEX
          I like winning dance contests. Like
          the one I'm going to win tonight.

                    WILLY
          Please. After I beat you in tonight's
          contest, I can have any woman in the
          Savoy I want. Come help me pick out my
          harem.

                    ALEX
          Women can wait, Willy. Let's say hello
          to Curtis.

ALEX AND WILLY

walk across the ballroom over to the 141ST STREET SIDE of the
ballroom where Curtis's pre-ordained booth lies in the

CAT'S CORNER

Curtis is accompanied by Big Mabel, Geraldine, Richard, and
Little Sally.

Curtis's arm is intimately wrapped around Geraldine.

                    CURTIS
          Washington, you boys really entering
          the contest?

                    ALEX
          I'm no Curtis Moore, but I think it
          will be a good experience.

                    CURTIS
          I'm really getting tired of winning
          every year. Maybe, I should just
          retire.

                    RICHARD
          I've got a pretty unique Swingout this
          year. Maybe I'll win?

                    WILLY
          We've got some really tight moves, too.
          I wouldn't--

                    ALEX
          Everyone knows you're the champ,
          Curtis.

                    GERALDINE
          If he's not, I'm with the wrong guy.

Everyone around the table SNICKERS.

                    ALEX
          I'd like to talk with you after the
          contest.

                    CURTIS
          You know where to find me.

Alex and Willy leave Curtis.

140TH STREET STAGE

They find FREDA AND MARGARET waiting for them in the spot where
they separated.

                    ALEX
          Let's Lindy.

                    FREDA
          I don't feel like dancing right now.

                    ALEX
          You wanted to dance ten minutes ago.

                    FREDA
          That was ten minutes ago.

                    ALEX
          Don't start with me. I could be
          dancing with any girl I please, but
          I've chosen you.

                    FREDA
          I asked you to be my partner.

141ST STREET STAGE

The MUSIC stops. MR. BUCHANAN, now 52-years-old, walks onto
the stage in front of a microphone.

Swingout

BOUCNERS

rope off an area in the CAT'S CORNER.

> MR. BUCHANAN
> Ladies and Gentlemen. Lenny's Lindy
> Hoppers.

JAMES GRANT & EYDIE HAYES (20-years-old), and AL JONES (18-years-old) & IDA MILLER (17-years-old) take the floor.

They're all African-Americans and around Alex's age.

They perform a simple, but entertaining routine.

The audience applauds.

> MR. BUCHANAN
> And now let's begin the final night of
> round one in the 10th Annual Harvest
> Moon Swingout.

LATER

THE JIMMIE LUNCEFORD ORCHESTRA

plays up-tempo music on the 141ST STREET STAGE.

A mediocre Lindy Hop couple makes a sloppy attempt to show their stuff.

ALEX

yawns while he Freda, Willy, and Margaret impatiently wait their turn.

> WILLY
> Bet you dinner at Small's we get more
> applause than you.

> ALEX
> Yeah, right.

> FREDA
> Chicken?

> MARGARET
> You're on.

The mediocre couple finishes.

Applause of courtesy.

                         MR. BUCHANAN
              Our next couple is Willy and Margaret.

WILLY AND MARGARET

Swingout onto the dance floor.

They put on an incredible performance.

AS WILLY AND MARGARET

leave the dance floor they snap their FINGERS in unison at

Alex and Freda

                         FREDA
              Oh, hell no. Are you going to take
              that?

                         MR. BUCHANAN
              And our last couple is Alex and Freda.

                         ALEX
              A one, a two, you know what to do.

ALEX AND FREDA

Swingout onto the dance floor.

They are good, but they aren't getting the same reaction Willy
and Margaret got.

Alex improvises.

                         FREDA
              I don't know what you're doing.

                         ALEX
              I'm feeling the moment. Just follow my
              lead.

FREDA

is frustrated.

                         FREDA
              Stick with what we know.

                         ALEX
              Just shut-up and dance.

Freda breaks away from Alex.

Swingout

Freestyles taunting Alex to come after her.

The crowd loves it.

                    ALEX
          Damnit Freda, what are you doing?

                    FREDA
          I'm feeling the moment.

ALEX SNATCHES FREDA

They Swingout into a daredevil AIRSTEP no-one has ever seen
before.

                    WILLY / MARGARET
          Shit.

She almost falls, but Alex catches her and it appears as though
it was part of the move.

The crowd goes insane with applause.

                    BILLIE HOLIDAY
          He's good.

                    BIG MABEL
          Look at how good Alex is, Curtis.

The music stops and Freda breaks away from Alex and storms off
of the floor.

                    CURTIS (V.O.)
          But, Alex wasn't good -- he was great.
          For the first time in nearly 20 years
          of dancing, I was afraid.

ALEX

more than plays it off by taking a few solo bows.

                    MARGARET
          Are you all right, baby?

                    FREDA
          He's such a conceited bastard?

                    WILLY
          Where in the hell did you get that
          airstep?

ALEX

points to his heart.

> ALEX
> It's in here.

> MR. BUCHANAN
> Would all of the couples please line
> up?

Six couples including Alex & Freda and Willy & Margaret line up
in the middle of

CAT'S CORNER

> MR. BUCHANAN (CONT'D)
> By round of applause, will it be Sam &
> Linda, George & Bethenia, Etta &
> Monroe, Fats and Gertrude, Willy &
> Margaret--

The audience reacts with loud SCREAMS.

> MR. BUCHANAN (CONT'D)
> Or Alex and Freda.

The audience reacts with equal applause to Willy and Margaret.

> MR. BUCHANAN
> I believe we have our last two finalist
> couples for the first round of the
> Harvest Moon Swingout: Willy & Margaret
> and Alex & Freda.

WILLY AND MARGARET

run out onto the dance floor hand in hand.

ALEX GRABS FREDA'S HAND,

but she yanks it away from him and prances out by herself.

ALEX

plays on her move, and does not move pretending to give his
lady all the credit.

He casually takes his place near her.

> MARGARET
> We had more applause.

Swingout

                    ALEX
What are you talking about? We had
more applause.

                    WILLY
They called us first.

                    FREDA
They saved the best for last.

                    ALEX
I'll be right back, I've got talk to
Curtis.

Alex walks over to

CURTIS'S BOOTH

                    CURTIS
You're getting better.

                    GERALDINE
You were wonderful.

                    ALEX
That's what I want to talk to you
about. I want to join your dance team.

                    LITTLE SALLY
You're still not Curtis.

                    CURTIS
Can we discuss this later?

                    ALEX
I've waited a long time for this
moment.

                    CURTIS
You're not ready.

                    BIG MABEL
Curtis, what's the big deal. We just
dance. He'll be fine.

                    ALEX
Did you hear the crowd? I won.

                    CURTIS
You won a battle, son. Not the war.
All the Lindy Hoppers on my team have
proven themselves over the years.

                         RICHARD
          I noticed he has his own Swingout.

                         CURTIS
          My mind is made up. Maybe next year.

Alex gets in Curtis's face.

                         ALEX
          Why not now? I'm good. Hell, I might
          even beat you.

                         CURTIS
          That's what I'm talking about. You're
          too cocky.

CURTIS

sticks his finger hard into Alex's chest.

                         CURTIS (CONT'D)
          You don't know your place.

                         GERALDINE
          I think that's enough.

                         ALEX
          You don't know your place.

ALEX

pushes CURTIS'S HAND off of his chest.

                         ALEX (CONT'D)
          People talk. They say you're getting
          old and there are a lot of new Lindy
          Hoppers with new moves. People are
          saying you might not win the Harvest
          Moon this year.

                         CURTIS
          And who will, you?

Curtis shoves Alex.

                         GERALDINE
          Moore, that's enough.

                         CURTIS
          Shut up!

                        ALEX
             Maybe I will.

Alex

pushes on Curtis, but he doesn't budge.

                        CURTIS
             You can't beat me.

                        GERALDINE
             Walk away, Alex.

                        ALEX
             I'll see you in the finals, old man.

ALEX

leaves the table.

CURTIS

puts his arm around Geraldine.

                        CURTIS (V.O.)
             And he couldn't beat me. At least not
             that night. Alex was a natural. He
             never practiced. With a little polish,
             I knew he could beat me.

GERALDINE'S EYES study

ALEX

as he boldly leaves the booth.

ALEX

storms back over to the

140TH STREET STAGE

where Willy, Freda, and Margaret are waiting for him with Mr.
Buchanan.

                        MR. BUCHANAN
             I need you kids to come backstage to
             get some information about round two.

ALEX, FREDA, WILLY, AND MARGARET

take a victory stroll

backstage

with Mr. Buchanan.

BILLIE HOLIDAY

walks towards her dressing room and notices Alex.

Billie Holiday touches him on the shoulder.

                    BILLIE HOLIDAY
        I like your Swingout.

                    ALEX
        Thanks, Ms. Holiday.

                    BILLIE HOLIDAY
        Please don't say that. I'm just as old
        as you are. Call me Billie.

LENNY

steps backstage unnoticed.

He catches a glimpse of Billie Holiday talking to Alex and
lends an ear.

                    ALEX
        Thanks, Billie.

                    BILLIE HOLIDAY
        My manager thinks we should add Lindy
        Hoppers to my show. Do you have a
        manager?

                    ALEX
        No, but Ms. Clarke in the front office
        always knows how to get in contact with
        me.

                    BILLIE HOLIDAY
        See you soon.

BILLIE HOLIDAY

steps into her dressing room.

                    ALEX
          Since Freda is in a tiff, let's call it
          an evening.

                    FREDA
          Actually, I want to stay and dance.

                    WILLY
          There they go again.

                    MARGARET
          You two have really got it bad.

Alex, Freda, Willy, and Margaret walk back into the

BALLROOM

Lenny slithers behind them.

                    LENNY
          Alex, can I talk to you for a moment,
          alone? It's business

                    ALEX
          Decide what we're going to do. I'll
          catch up with y'all in a minute.

FREDA, WILLY, AND MARGARET

move along and argue about how to proceed with the evening.

                    LENNY
          Nice performance. I like your
          Swingout.

                    ALEX
          Thanks.

                    LENNY
          I want you and Freda to join my dance
          team.

                    ALEX
          No thanks.

                    LENNY
          Some of the best kids in town are on my
          team. You should be flattered.

                    ALEX
          Kids. I'm an advanced dancer. Freda
          and I get enough gigs on our own.

                         LENNY
              I only have room for one more couple.
              I'll give you a day to think it over,
              and then I'm going to offer the spot to
              somebody else.

Lenny walks away.

EXT. SAVOY - ALLEY - NIGHT

Curtis and a FLOOZY make out against the wall.

INT. SAVOY - BACKSTAGE - NIGHT

GERALDINE wanders backstage towards the LADIES ROOM.

She notices the back door is AJAR.

Walks towards door.

Overhears intense MOANS OF PASSION.

EXT. SAVOY - ALLEY - NIGHT

Curtis and the Floozy are CAUGHT IN THE ACT.

                         GERALDINE
              That's the last time you'll fuck- me or
              my money.

Geraldine charges back inside.

                         CURTIS
              Geraldine. No, wait. Let me explain.

The Floozy drops to her knees.

                         CURTIS
              I'll be there in just a moment.

INT. SAVOY - NIGHT

Alex wanders over to the

140TH STREET STAGE

to look for his friends.

Swingout

Geraldine grabs Alex.

ALEX
Tell Curtis I haven't a God damn thing to say to him.

GERALDINE
Neither do I. I'm buying you a drink.

ALEX
I think the gang is going out, but I don't know how much celebrating we'll be doing.

Alex's friends rush over to him.

FREDA,

sensing female competition from Geraldine, instinctively links arms with Alex.

FREDA
Come on, Washington. You're slowing us down. We want to go to Small's.

GERALDINE
Alex's with me.

Alex

links arms with Geraldine.

ALEX
Geraldine and I are going out alone.

MARGARET
Oooooooooooooooooo.

ALEX
Later children.

FREDA
At least we don't have to worry about you spoiling our fun.

ALEX AND GERALDINE

prance away.

FREDA

keeps her EYES focused on Alex and Geraldine.

INT. RESTAURANT — NIGHT

ALEX AND GERALDINE chat over a couple of slices of cheesecake and Irish coffee.

ALEX chuckles.

>   GERALDINE
>   What's so funny?

>   ALEX
>   It's just that over the years when you
>   would see Curtis in between production
>   of your films, we would talk, but we
>   never really talked.

>   GERALDINE
>   There's a time and a place for
>   everything.

GERALDINE

seductively puts her LIPS onto her glass.

Takes a SMALL PACKAGE out of her purse and hands it to Alex.

>   GERALDINE
>   Take this.

>   ALEX
>   What is it?

>   GERALDINE
>   It's a small present from me to you.

>   ALEX
>   I can't accept this.

>   GERALDINE
>   Think of it as a victory gift.

Alex accepts the gift.

>   GERALDINE
>   Don't open it until you get home.

                    ALEX
This is not right. I shouldn't be
hanging out with Curtis's girl.

                  GERALDINE
I was never Curtis's girl, he was my
man. And for your information, I fired
him. I'm a single, wealthy adult and
I'll do damn well as I please.

                    ALEX
I really enjoyed this evening.

                  GERALDINE
Then I'll take it as guarantee we'll
get together again.

                    ALEX
No guarantees.

Geraldine raises her coffee cup for a toast.

                  GERALDINE
To the future.

                    ALEX
The future.

Their COFFEE CUPS meet.

                                    MATCHCUT TO:

INT. ALEX'S APARTMENT — DAY

Alex places two COFFEE CUPS on a TRAY amongst a breakfast
setting for two.

He carries the tray towards a large curtain.

                    ALEX
Knock, knock.

                  FEMALE VOICE
Who's there?

                    ALEX
Breakfast in bed.

                  FEMALE VOICE
Come in.

Alex pulls the curtain back and walks into the

BEDROOM

where MOTHER WASHINGTON, 48-years-old, awakens.

>   MOTHER WASHINGTON
>   Whatever it is, bribery will get you
>   nowhere.

>   ALEX
>   Can't a son do something for his mother
>   because he loves her?

Alex

places the tray of food down in front of Mother Washington.

>   MOTHER WASHINGTON
>   No. You stayed out all night dancing,
>   didn't you?

>   ALEX
>   I won last night, Mama.

>   MOTHER WASHINGTON
>   Swing dancing is not a career, Alex.
>   How do you plan to raise a family? You
>   need to go see Mr. Fitzgerald and get a
>   job down at the Post Office. You can
>   build a happy life with a career like
>   that.

Mother Washington eats her breakfast.

>   ALEX
>   You should have been there last night.
>   The crowd loved me.

Alex

steps out of the bedroom area and grabs the PACKAGE Geraldine
gave him.

He opens it and it's full of MONEY.

>   MOTHER WASHINGTON
>   Where did you get all the money?

>   ALEX
>   Dancing...It's prize money.

                    MOTHER WASHINGTON
          Are you involved with those gangsters?
          I swear I'll kill you before they do.

                         ALEX
          No, Mama. I got it...dancing. And
          when I win $5,000 dollars in the finals
          of this year's Harvest Moon Swingout,
          I'll be the King of Swing. Everything
          is going to be just fine for now on.

Alex KISSES Mother Washington on the cheek.

Mother Washington pulls away.

                    MOTHER WASHINGTON
          When you get a job at the Post Office
          is when everything is going to be just
          fine.

                         ALEX
          Trust me.

INT. ALEX'S APARTMENT BUILDING — DAY

ALEX walks through the hallway.

Stops at a door.

Knocks on it.

After a beat, the door opens, and MRS. WASHINGTON, a 48-year-
old African-American woman, opens the door.

                    MRS. WASHINGTON
          No. You're all ready three months
          behind. If you can't pay you can't
          stay. I've done all I can, but if I
          don't get money from you, Mr. Myer is
          going to put me out, too.

Alex hands Mrs. Washington a wad of MONEY. Mrs. Washington
counts the money.

                    MRS. WASHINGTON
          It's all here. I don't ask questions
          or get involved. Just don't bring any
          trouble in the building.

                              ALEX
                    Good afternoon, Mrs. Washington. And
                    how are you today?

Mrs. Washington closes her door.

EXT. GARMENT FACTORY — DAY

Lenny walks into a fabric sweat shop.

INT. GARMENT FACTORY - DAY

Freda works amongst several rows of SEAMSTRESSES sewing
together men's sport coats.

Lenny

speaks to, MRS. BRANDT, a 44-year-old Caucasian woman who
appears to be in charge.

She points to FREDA and holds up FIVE FINGERS to Lenny.

Lenny walks over to Freda.

                              LENNY
                    Freda, I need to speak with you alone
                    outside.

                              FREDA
                    Can't it wait till later, I need my
                    job?

                              LENNY
                    It's business.

Freda

begrudgingly stops her work and follows Lenny outside.

As Freda passes Mrs. Brandt, Mrs. Brandt holds up FIVE FINGERS.

EXT. GARMENT FACTORY - DAY

Lenny and Freda step outside of the factory.

Freda

takes a seat on a stoop.

Lenny
Swingout

leans against a light post.

>   LENNY
>   I want you and Alex to join my team.

>   FREDA
>   How much are you going to pay us?

>   LENNY
>   Never mind, I changed my mind.

Lenny walks away.

Freda hops up and grabs Lenny's arm.

>   FREDA
>   Wait.

>   LENNY
>   I talked to Alex, but he wasn't
>   completely sold on the idea.

>   FREDA
>   What do you want from me?

>   LENNY
>   My kids have been getting a lot of
>   gigs, lately. More than we can
>   fulfill. As a matter of fact, I have
>   one this Wednesday, but no available
>   Lindy Hoppers.

>   FREDA
>   Will it interfere with my day job?

>   LENNY
>   Swing is the future. I have big plans
>   for the team. I guess I was wrong
>   about you. I can see you already have
>   a future right here.

>   FREDA
>   If Alex doesn't want to do it, there's
>   nothing I can do.

>   LENNY
>   Maybe I should have someone else dance
>   with Alex. You two really don't get
>   along well anyway and most partners end
>   up falling in love with each other. I
>   wouldn't want to wish that on you.
>   Sorry I disturbed you. Good luck.

Lenny walks away from Freda.

INT. GARMENT FACTORY - DAY

Freda slowly walks back to her sewing machine.

MRS. BRANDT

motions for Freda to hurry it up.

FREDA

sits at her sewing machine staring at the SPORT COAT she was
sewing.

                              MATCHCUT TO:

INT. MEN'S CLOTHING STORE - DAY

Geraldine grabs a SPORT COAT off of a rack and hands it to
Alex.

                    GERALDINE
          Try it on.

                    ALEX
          No, it's all right.

                    GERALDINE
          Try it on.

Alex tries on the coat.

Geraldine affectionately straightens the sport coat on Alex.

                    GERALDINE
          Do you like it?

                    ALEX
          It's nice, but I'm not buying any suits
          today.

                    GERALDINE
          I am.

Geraldine catches a SALESPERSON's attention.

                    GERALDINE
          We'll take it.

Swingout

                    ALEX
          No, we won't. I can't accept this.

                    GERALDINE
          It's better to give than receive. If
          you want to win the Harvest Moon
          Swingout, you just can't wear anything.
          You've got to be clean. Think of it as
          doing me a favor.

                    ALEX
          Looking at the price tag, it looks like
          I've done you a big favor.

EXT. SHOE STORE - DAY

ALEX AND GERALDINE,

arms full of bags, walk into the store.

INT. SHOE STORE - DAY

Geraldine sits next to Alex.

A SHOE SALESMAN brings Alex a box of shoes.

                    SHOE SALESMAN
          Dancing shoes.

The Shoe Salesman walks away.

Alex takes off his shoes.

                    GERALDINE
          I know the most darling little night
          club we can go to this evening.

                    ALEX
          I'm sorry Geraldine, I have plans.

ALEX

opens the box and takes out a shoe.

                    GERALDINE
          Cancel them.

                    ALEX
          Freda and I are going dancing at the
          Savoy with Margaret and Willy.

                         GERALDINE
          Why spend time with a girl when you can
          be with a woman.

Alex tries on the shoes.

                         ALEX
          Freda's my partner. It's good business
          for us to be seen dancing together.

                         GERALDINE
          I thought this was the beginning of an
          interesting arrangement between the two
          of us.

                         ALEX
          Maybe another night this week.

EXT. SAVOY BALLROOM — NIGHT

Teenagers Lindy Hop to BIG BAND MUSIC roaring into the streets.

MARQUEE

"COUNT BASIE FEATURING JOE JAMESS AND LUCKY MILLANDER."

INT. SAVOY BALLROOM - NIGHT

THE LUCKY MILLANDER BAND plays on the

140TH STREET STAGE

As Lindy Hoppers leave the floor,

ALEX AND FREDA

Swingout onto the dance floor, then

WILLY AND MARGARET

                         ALEX
          This band is really Swinging.

                         FREDA
          Alex, I've been thinking it might be
          good for us to dance on a team.

Alex stops dancing.

Swingout

                         ALEX
          Lenny talked to you, didn't he?

                         FREDA
          What does that have to do with
          anything?

                         ALEX
          All his Lindy Hoppers are unknowns.

                         FREDA
          What about Goody? He's been around
          awhile?

                         ALEX
          What about Goody? He's yesterday's
          news.

                         FREDA
          You say you want to win the Harvest
          Moon Swingout, but you're not willing
          to do anything to win it.

Willy and Margaret playfully Swingout between

ALEX AND FREDA

                         MARGARET
          Excuse us.

                         WILLY
          The dance floor is for dancing not
          standing and talking.

Alex tries to lead Freda off of the floor by her arm, but she
jerks it away.

                         FREDA
          Get your hands off of me.

ALEX AND FREDA

walk off of the dance floor into the

DINING AREA

and take a seat at a table.

                         ALEX
          What is your problem?

                          FREDA
            If we were on Lenny's team, we'd
            probably get more gigs, make some extra
            money, and get some exposure dancing in
            his silly little 400 Club Cat's Corner.

                          ALEX
            Fine. Then we'll join his damn team.
            Happy?

                          FREDA
            I don't want to join the dance team.

WILLY AND MARGARET

walk over to the table.

                          ALEX
            What is it with you? If I jumped off a
            bridge, you'd jump on the bridge. If I
            jumped on the bridge, you'd jump off
            the bridge.

                          FREDA
            You don't know how to talk to people.
            I'm leaving.

Freda asks a DRUNK MAN to dance.

They pounce onto the dance floor of the

141st Street Side

                          MARGARET
            What's wrong?

                          ALEX
            Lenny asked us to dance on his team.

                          WILLY
            That's cool. It's hard to get on his
            team. Congratulations.

                          ALEX
            I said no and she said yes, then I said
            yes, and she said no--

Willy notices Freda is dancing with a

DRUNK

He's out of control, stepping on her.

Swingout

                    WILLY
          You better go get your woman. She's
          dancing with a dangerous person.

Alex storms over to the

141ST STREET SIDE

dance floor. He grabs the Drunk by the SHOULDER.

                    ALEX
          Excuse me, that's my partner.

The drunk pushes Alex.

                    DRUNK
          Back off. She asked me to dance first.

ALEX

punches the Drunk and knocks him down.

A BIG GOON sees this.

                    BIG GOON
          Hey, that's my boy.

The Big Goon TACKLES Alex.

                    WILLY
          Shit.

Alex BREAKS AWAY from him.

BIG GOON

picks up a CHAIR, but Willy plants a punch right in his gut.

The Big Goon's knees buckle.

Lenny

rushes over with several BOUNCERS.

                    LENNY
          Washington, these guys bothering you?

                    ALEX
          This drunk fool put my girl in
          jeopardy.

                    LENNY
          You stupid drunkards are banned from
          the Savoy. Get these idiots out of
          here.

BOUNCERS

DRAG the Drunk and Big Goon away.

                    LENNY
          Take my handkerchief, your lip is
          bleeding.

FREDA

takes the handkerchief and NURSES Alex's wound.

                    ALEX
          Freda and I have decided to join your
          dance team, but under one condition--

ALEX

puts his arms around WILLY AND MARGARET.

                    ALEX (CONT'D)
          You take my friends, too.

                    LENNY
          I only need one more couple right now.

                    ALEX
          Then forget it.

ALEX

walks away with Freda, Willy, and Margaret to the 141ST STREET
STAGE.

THE LUCKY MILLANDER ORCHESTRA FINISHES PLAYING ON THE 140TH
STREET STAGE.

THE COUNT BASIE ORCHESTRA plays a really Swinging up-tempo tune
on the 141ST STREET STAGE.

                    FREDA
          It's been too much excitement for one
          night. Let's leave.

                    ALEX
          No, let's Lindy.

Swingout

ALEX AND FREDA

Swingout onto the dance floor.

WILLY DRAGS MARGARET

away from Alex and Freda.

Willy and Margaret clap for Alex and Freda.

ALEX AND FREDA

start to show out in rare form.

A full-fledged

JAM CIRCLE

clears for Alex and Freda.

Alex and Freda leap out of the circle next to

WILLY AND MARGARET

                    ALEX / FREDA
          Tag!

WILLY AND MARGARET

Swingout onto the dance floor.

Willy and Margaret give Alex and Freda a run for the money.

WILLY CARRIES MARGARET

off of the dance floor and TAGS Alex.

ALEX AND FREDA

Swingout back into the dance floor.

LENNY

watches from afar.

He likes what he sees.

Alex notices Lenny watching.

                    ALEX
          Freestyle!

Alex BREAKS AWAY from Freda.

They Freestyle.

Alex reclaims Freda. He Swings her out to

WILLY

who takes the dance floor and Lindy Hops with Freda.

ALEX

grabs Margaret. They Swingout onto the dance floor.

Alex and Willy every few phrases Swing their girl out to each
other and switch partners.

The Savoy crowd eats it up and so does LENNY.

The MUSIC STOPS.

ALEX, FREDA, MARGARET, AND WILLY

collapse on top of each other in the floor.

                    TOM GATES
                (into mic)
         Damn, them kids can Swing.

Lenny

approaches Alex and his friends.

                    LENNY
        All right kids, you win. You're all on
        the team.

Alex, Freda, Willy, and Margaret all slap each other five.

Lenny puts his arm around Alex.

                    LENNY
        Son, cancel your plans Wednesday night.

EXT. SAVOY BALLROOM — DAY

A car stops in front of the Savoy.

ALEX

gets out of the car and waves good-bye to the driver who is
GERALDINE.

INT. SAVOY BALLROOM - DAY

THE GLENN ALLEYNE ORCHESTRA rehearses on the stage.

GOODY LESTER, a 38-year-old African-American dancer, performs a
routine with Freda, Willy & Margaret, James & Eydie, and Bubba
& Ida.

ALEX

casually strolls into the ballroom like a King.

He takes a seat, plops his feet on a table, and watches each
couple dance through their solo part once.

>   GOODY
> So, nice of the King of Swing to join
> us. I guess you didn't think my
> routine was worthy of you.

>   FREDA
> Alex, you're over an hour late.

>   ALEX
> Time must have gotten away from me.

CURTIS

sticks his head out from behind backstage unnoticed.

>   JAMES
> You're lucky Lenny didn't get here,
> yet. He hates it when people aren't
> team players.

>   GOODY
> Watch it a few more times, Alex, and
> then I'll try and break it down for
> you.

>   ALEX
> I've I already got the routine down.

>   GOODY
> Which couple's routine?

                    ALEX
          All of them.

                    GOODY
          You memorized all of the routines by
          just watching them once.

                    ALEX
          Yes.

                    GOODY
          Why not provide us with a demonstration
          then, Jesus of the dance floor?

Alex

takes Freda's, HAND. They Swingout onto the dance floor.

                    ALEX
          This one is James and Eydie's routine.

Alex executes the routine flawlessly.

                    ALEX
          This one is Bubba and Ida's.

Alex continues to dance the routines perfectly without missing
a beat.

                    ALEX
          This one is Willy's and Margaret's.

Alex EMBELLISHES a little.

                    WILLY
          Showoff.

                    ALEX
          And this one is yours and Freda's.

MOUTHS hang wide open.

                    ALEX
          But the Swingout into Back CHARLESTON
          doesn't really work. What about a
          Swingout with a Half-Spin into an Over-
          The-Back?

Alex executes his new combination and all of the Lindy Hoppers,
except Goody, CLAP.

Alex an Freda stop dancing.

Swingout

> IDA
> Alex, teach us something that will make
> us famous.

> EVERYONE (EXCEPT GOODY)
> Yeah, teach us some new stuff.

> ALEX
> No-no, what you have is OK.

> EYDIE
> We'll never see anything else besides
> Harlem doing the same old thing.
> Please.

CURTIS

lurks in the SHADOWS.

Stares at Alex.

> CURTIS (V.O.)
> Genius. Genius. Sheer Genius. Alex
> Washington was everything I ever wanted
> to be and more.

Dances with an imaginary partner.

> CURTIS (V.O.) (CONT'D)
> I had trained and practiced all my life
> and this kid could execute intricate
> moves without even thinking about it.
> It was as if God himself had taken
> control of his body. He didn't deserve
> it. I was the King of Swing.

Curtis chokes his imaginary partner.

Shakes his fists at God.

> CURTIS (V.O.) (CONT'D)
> All those afternoons he spent with me
> after school were only to study me like
> a blueprint. Alex Washington was no
> longer my student. He was my enemy.

EXT. SAVOY BALLROOM — DAY

CURTIS storms out of the front door fuming not noticing Lenny
entering through the same door.

Curtis walks directly INTO Lenny.

                    LENNY
          Watch out there guy.

                    CURTIS
          You know your new little hot shot is in
          there trying to take over your team.

                    LENNY
          What are you talking about?

                    CURTIS
          He's teaching a new routine.

                    LENNY
          Alex's got a lot of good moves.

                    CURTIS
          Use your instincts. Read between the
          lines. Makes no difference to me. I
          have my own dance team.

CURTIS

walks away from Lenny and down the street.

INT. SAVOY BALLROOM - DAY

Alex choreographs the Lindy Hoppers.

They look unbelievably better.

LENNY

walks into the ballroom area.

The Lindy Hoppers complete their routine.

                    BUBBA
          Lenny, check out this new routine Alex
          taught us. We could make a lot of
          money.

                    IDA
          We could all become stars.

Swingout

                    LENNY
          There will be no new routines until I
          say there are. I can't believe you
          participated in this, Goody. You're no
          better than these silly kids.

                    ALEX
          Fine, then. Lose it, don't use it.

EXT. SAVOY BALLROOM - NIGHT

An endless line wraps around the block.

MARQUEE

"DUKE ELLINGTON & FRANK SINATRA."

INT. SAVOY BALLROOM - NIGHT

THE DUKE ELLINGTON ORCHESTRA plays on the 141ST STREET STAGE.

Alex and Freda Lindy Hop in the

CAT'S CORNER

along with Willy & Margaret, James & Eydie, and Bubba & Ida.

THE DUKE ELLINGTON ORCHESTRA plays a really Swinging up-tempo
tune.

LENNY

walks amongst his Lindy Hoppers surveying their moves.

                    LENNY
          Form a Jam circle.

Jam circle

Bubba and Ida Swingout into the jam circle.

When they finish, Willy and Margaret Swingout then James and
Eydie.

TODD SMITH,

a 45-year-old Caucasian man, and manager of the Cotton Club,
watches Lenny's Lindy Hoppers with amazement.

ALEX AND FREDA

dance last and win the crowd over.

Todd approaches Lenny.

CURTIS & BIG MABEL and RICHARD & LITTLE SALLY

Lindy Hop nearby.

Curtis recognizes TODD.

Tries to eavesdrop.

>   TODD
>   I'm short one act and I'd like your
>   Lindy Hoppers to do a routine at the
>   Cotton Club tomorrow night.

Curtis scoffs. Stops dancing.

EXT. ALEX'S APARTMENT BUILDING — DAY

Alex walks into the building carrying groceries.

INT. ALEX'S APARTMENT - DAY

Mother Washington walks out of the bedroom in a robe and
slippers.

Alex

enters the apartment.

>   ALEX
>   Good morning. I was hoping to get back
>   before you woke.

>   MOTHER WASHINGTON
>   Out all night again. I don't know how
>   you do it.

>   ALEX
>   You're never going to believe this.

>   MOTHER WASHINGTON
>   What is it this time?

                    ALEX
Lenny got the team booked at the Cotton
Club.

                MOTHER WASHINGTON
You really don't need to be around
those seedy showgirls at the Cotton
Club.

                    ALEX
It's not like that at all.

                MOTHER WASHINGTON
Lots of gangsters go to that place,
too.

                    ALEX
You worry too much.

                MOTHER WASHINGTON
That's right. And if you don't see Mr.
Fitzgerald and get a job at the Post
Office, you're going to worry your poor
old mother to death. That is, if I
don't starve first.

                    ALEX
Trust me.

EXT. COTTON CLUB — NIGHT

Fancy cars and fancy Caucasian patrons stand eager and
impatient in line.

INT. COTTON CLUB - BACKSTAGE - NIGHT

James, Eydie, Willy, Margaret, Bubba, Ida, Freda, and Lenny
wait impatiently backstage.

                    LENNY
        Where is he?

                    FREDA
        I don't know. I'm not his keeper.

Todd

walks over to the group.

                    TODD
          Lenny's Lindy Hoppers, you're on in
          five minutes.

                    LENNY
          Todd, one of our guys got caught in
          traffic. Can you move our act?

                    TODD
          No. You're on in five. You'll have to
          dance without him. The show must go
          on.

                    FREDA
          Lenny, why don't you dance with me?

                    LENNY
          I don't Lindy.

Lenny stares at his

WATCH HANDS

"9:55 P.M."

                                   MATCHCUT TO:

INT. APARTMENT - NIGHT

CLOCK HANDS

"9:55 P.M."

wobble rhythmically on a nightstand.

ALEX AND GERALDINE

engage in INTENSE SEX tearing the bed apart until they climax
together with complimentary cries of ecstasy.

Through Geraldine's bedroom

WINDOW

a car parks in front of the building.

                                   SLOW ZOOM TO:

Swingout

EXT. GERALDINE'S APARTMENT BUILDING - NIGHT

CURTIS

turns of the ignition of the car now parked in front of the building.

INT. GERALDINE'S APARTMENT - NIGHT

Alex rolls off of Geraldine.

Geraldine puts her LIPS to his EAR.

> GERALDINE
> I found your new dance partner.

> ALEX
> What are you talking about? I already have one. It's Freda.

> GERALDINE
> But, you two always argue. She doesn't appreciate you. You'll love Mary. She's wonderful.

> ALEX
> But, Freda...oh shit. What time is it?

Alex

leaps out of the bed and grabs the

CLOCK

"9:57 P.M."

> ALEX
> God, help me. I'm supposed to be dancing at the Cotton Club right now.

Geraldine sits up in bed.

Alex grabs his clothes.

> ALEX
> I gotta' go.

54.

ALEX

runs out of the bedroom.

INT. CAR - NIGHT

Curtis picks up a dozen ROSES from the passenger's seat.

EXT. GERALDINE'S APARTMENT BUILDING - NIGHT

Curtis sees Alex run out of the building and down the street.

INT. HALLWAY - NIGHT

Curtis knocks on Geraldine's door.

INT. APARTMENT - NIGHT

Geraldine rolls out of bed naked.

Drapes a sheet over her.

                    GERALDINE
          I thought you were going to—

INT. HALLWAY - NIGHT

Geraldine opens her door.

Curtis stands before her.

                    GERALDINE
          The Cotton Club.

                    CURTIS
          Mother fucker.

EXT. STREET - NIGHT

Curtis drives like a wild maniac.

EXT. COTTON CLUB — BACKSTAGE - NIGHT

LENNY stands outside paying his Lindy Hoppers.

Swingout

He gives James and Eydie some MONEY.

ALEX

runs up to Lenny.

> ALEX
> I'm so sorry. I got tied up. Did I
> miss it?

Lenny PAYS Willy & Margaret and Bubba & Ida.

> LENNY
> Sorry, Freda. He only paid me for the
> amount of couples who performed, but
> I'll give you some of my cut for
> showing up.

> FREDA
> That's OK.

> LENNY
> No, I insist. It won't happen again.

Freda

accepts the money.

> LENNY
> Washington, you're suspended.

> ALEX
> What do you mean, suspended? You can't
> suspend me, you need me.

> LENNY
> It's Lenny's Lindy Hoppers, kid. Not
> Alex's Lindy Hoppers. There's no room
> on the team for prima donnas.

> ALEX
> Fuck you then, I quit.

Curtis's car screeches into the alley.

CURTIS

leaps out of the car leaving his door wide open.

SLUGS Alex and knocks him down.

ALEX

gets up and tries to strike Curtis, but Curtis socks him in the stomach.

Alex

drops to his KNEES.

                    CURTIS
          Get up punk.

WILLY

attempts to assist Alex, but

Lenny

holds him back.

                    LENNY
          This is between those two men.

ALEX

tries to strike, but Curtis slugs him again and knocks him down.

                    LENNY
          That's enough, Curtis.

Curtis

stands Alex up and pushes him against the wall.

                    WILLY
          That's it.

WILLY

rushes Curtis, but

CURTIS

pulls out a SWITCHBLADE and holds it to Alex's THROAT.

WILLY

stops moving.

                    WILLY
          Easy now.

Swingout

                        CURTIS
            If you ever go near Geraldine again, I
            will kill you.

Curtis

throws Alex into Willy.

                        ALEX
            Fuck everybody.

Freda

reaches for Alex.

                        FREDA
            Alex.

Alex

pushes her hands off of him and walks away.

                        FREDA
            Alex.

                        LENNY
            Let him go.

Freda

runs after Alex.

LENNY

grabs her.

                        LENNY
            Don't.

EXT. SAVOY BALLROOM — DAY

Billie Holiday walks into the Savoy.

INT. SAVOY BALLROOM - DAY

THE SAVOY SULTANS rehearse on the stage.

Goody teaches James, Eydie, Bubba, Ida, and Freda a new routine
while Lenny observes.

58.

Billie Holiday takes a seat next to Lenny.

                    BILLIE HOLIDAY
          I need some Lindy Hoppers.

Rehearsal ceases at the sight of Billie Holiday.

                    LENNY
          When and where?

                    BILLIE HOLIDAY
          Actually, I came looking for that Alex
          fellow. Ms. Clarke told me he dances
          on your team, so I figured a team would
          be nice, too.

                    LENNY
          Alex is pretty busy right now. All of
          my Lindy Hoppers are just as amazing.

                    BILLIE HOLIDAY
          I'll take four couples, but only if
          Alex is included. The gig is in
          Boston.

EXT. ALEX'S APARTMENT BUILDING - DAY

Freda walks into the building.

INT. ALEX'S APARTMENT - DAY

Alex lies on the couch with a TOWEL filled with ice on his
face.

MOTHER WASHINGTON

lies in her bed with the curtain drawn.

KNOCKS resound from the door.

ALEX

drags himself off of the couch.

Opens the door.

                    ALEX
          What do you want?

Swingout

                    FREDA
          We need to talk.

                    MOTHER WASHINGTON (V.O.)
          Who's at the door?

                    ALEX
          It's the police. They've come to ask
          me some questions about the thugs who
          mugged me last night.

                    MOTHER WASHINGTON (V.O.)
          I told you there were gangsters at the
          Cotton Club.

Alex pushes Freda backwards away from the doorway.

INT. HALLWAY - DAY

Alex steps out of the apartment.

Closes the door behind him.

                    ALEX
          Didn't I tell you my mother is real
          sick and it's not good to come by?

                    FREDA
          Why weren't you in rehearsal today?

                    ALEX
          I'm a free agent. I don't work for any
          man.

                    FREDA
          We need you back. Billie Holiday wants
          us to dance in Boston.

                    ALEX
          Billie Holiday...but I don't dance for
          Lenny, anymore.

                    FREDA
          We can't do this without you.

                    ALEX
          Even if I did go back, I don't think he
          would let me dance.

                         FREDA
          Ah, yeah he would. He, uh, uh...that's
          all he talked about was getting you
          back.

                         ALEX
          Really.

                         FREDA
          Sure. Just come to rehearsal tomorrow
          and everything will be fine.

                         ALEX
          I knew he would come crawling back for
          me. I'll be in rehearsal tomorrow. I
          think we should change the name of the
          team to Alex's Lindy Hoppers, though.

                         FREDA
          Whatever. See you tomorrow.

                         ALEX
          Yes!

EXT. SAVOY BALLROOM — DAY

Alex and Freda walk into the Savoy.

INT. SAVOY BALLROOM - DAY

THE CHICK WEBB ORCHESTRA rehearses on stage.

Lenny and Goody sit at a table while James, Eydie, Willy,
Margaret, Bubba and Ida stretch.

Alex and Freda step onto the dance floor.

Lenny and Alex make EYE contact.

                         LENNY
          Looks like we're all here. Everyone
          line up. Goody is going to teach you a
          new routine for Billie Holiday in
          Boston. It's got to be good.

James steps close to Alex and whispers in his ear.

                         JAMES
          I'd say you just hit the lottery.
          Don't be a fool with your windfall.

Swingout

Alex and Freda line up with the rest of the Lindy Hoppers.

Lenny and Alex exchange HINTS OF SMILES.

EXT. AIRPORT — DAY

A large propeller airplane takes off.

EXT. HOTEL — BOSTON - NIGHT

Classy Caucasian customers leave their cars for the valet to park in front of the hotel.

MARQUEE

"BILLIE HOLIDAY."

INT. HOTEL - CLUB — BACKSTAGE - NIGHT

Alex, Freda, Willy, Margaret, Bubba, Ida, James, and Eydie all pace while watching SHOWGIRLS on stage.

None of the Lindy Hoppers are in costume.

>   FREDA
>   Where in the hell is Goody?

>   BUBBA
>   How long does it take to pick up
>   costumes? I hope they don't dock us
>   pay for this.

>   WILLY
>   I told y'all not to change your
>   costumes.

>   EYDIE
>   This is Billie Holiday. Everything has
>   to be just right or what's the point of
>   traveling here at all.

BILLIE HOLIDAY

comes backstage with Lenny's Lindy Hoppers.

>   BILLIE HOLIDAY
>   My manager just pointed out Kip Turner
>   in the audience.

                         IDA
          The big time Hollywood choreographer?
          He could make us famous.

Billie Holiday points through the curtains to KIP TURNER, 37-
year-old Caucasian male.

                    BILLIE HOLIDAY
          He's looking for Lindy Hoppers for his
          next film. Tonight might be your big
          break.

                         JAMES
          Has anyone heard from Goody? The team
          is counting on him.

THE STAGE MANAGER

walks over to Lenny's Lindy Hoppers.

                    STAGE MANAGER
          Lenny's Lindy Hoppers, you're on in
          five.

Walks away.

                    BILLIE HOLIDAY
          Nothing from Goody. Don't worry.
          You'll be fine. You're all terrific.

Billie Holiday walks away.

                         FREDA
          That's it. I can't do it.

                         ALEX
          What do you mean you can't do it?

                         FREDA
          Look at what I have on. Does this look
          terrific? That goofy routine is
          hopeless without us dressing alike.

                         JAMES
          You know she's right. We don't look
          like a team.

                         BUBBA
          James.

                    JAMES
          This is Billie Holiday and Kip Turner
          is in the audience. We need to be
          perfect. We need to do the routine
          Alex taught us.

                    EVERYONE
          Yeah. Let's do it.

                    ALEX
          Oh, no. Not with loose lips Goody
          lurking around.

                    IDA
          He's not here.

                    ALEX
          Yet.

                    IDA
          Lenny will never know.

                    ALEX
          No, no, no.

INT. HOTEL - CLUB - STAGE - NIGHT

The SHOWGIRLS finish their act and trot backstage.

INT. HOTEL - CLUB - BACKSTAGE - NIGHT

The Stage Manager runs over to Lenny's Lindy Hoppers.

                    STAGE MANAGER
          You're on!

                    JAMES
          What's it going to be?

Alex stands still deep in thought.

                    JAMES
          It's gotta' be one for all and all for
          one or not at all.

                    FREDA
          Please.

                         ALEX
              Let's show these people something they
              have never seen before.

Alex initiates a group handshake.

                         ALEX
              A one, a two, you know what to do?

                    STAGE MANAGER
              Hep, hep. Let's go.

Lenny's Lindy Hoppers sprint onto stage.

INT. HOTEL - CLUB - STAGE - NIGHT

Lenny's Lindy Hoppers dash into their places.

JAMES AND EYDIE dance first.

The crowd loves it.

Willy and Margaret dance next.

They are equally as breathtaking.

Bubba and Ida take over.

They are smothered by screams of euphoria.

INT. HOTEL - CLUB - BACKSTAGE - NIGHT

Goody arrives carrying the new costumes.

He is floored the team is doing Alex's routine.

                         GOODY
              Mother Fucker.

INT. HOTEL - CLUB - STAGE - NIGHT

Alex and Freda dance the last leg.

The crowd is speechless by their wonder.

For the grand finale, they do a unison airstep sequence that's
never been done before.

The crowd is so thrilled, Lenny's Lindy Hoppers are called back for

five encores

INT. HOTEL — LINDY HOPPERS' DRESSING ROOM - NIGHT

Lenny's Lindy Hoppers pour into the dressing room and celebrate.

Goody is silent.

> BUBBA
> We'll be the richest Lindy Hoppers in
> the world.

> IDA
> Nobody can Swing like Swingers from the
> Savoy.

A 43-year-old grumpy Caucasian male, Billie Holiday's Manager JOEL, bursts into the room.

> JOEL
> You're all fired.

> FREDA
> What?

> JOEL
> Five encores. You stopped the show.
> Nobody stops the show. This is the
> Billie Holiday show, not Lenny's Lindy
> Hoppers' show.

Joel storms out of the room and SLAMS the door.

> GOODY
> You should have recognized you needed
> to stick with my routine.

> ALEX
> Shut-up.

> GOODY
> I'm sick of you, boy.

GOODY

sucker punches Alex in the chest.

James and Willy grab Alex and Goody.

                    JAMES
          Hey, break it up. We're a team.

                    ALEX
          Hold on everyone. Everything is going
          to be OK. Trust me.

Alex runs out of the room.

INT. BILLIE HOLIDAY'S DRESSING ROOM - NIGHT

Billie Holiday and Joel stand toe-to-toe in a verbal brawl.

                    BILLIE HOLIDAY
          It's my show and I'll have whoever I
          want in it.

LOUD THUMPS emanate from the door.

                    ALEX (V.O.)
          Billie! Billie! Billie!

                    JOEL
          There were powerful important people
          who gave you your break.

                    BILLIE HOLIDAY
          If they're so important, Joel, then why
          not let them sing?

Alex kicks the door open.

                    ALEX
          Billie.

                    BILLIE HOLIDAY
          You're rehired. You're fired.

                    JOEL
          You can't fire me.

                    BILLIE HOLIDAY
          I just did. Get out.

Joel violently grabs Billie Holiday.

                    JOEL
          You're nothing but a two-bit singing
          monkey.

Swingout

Billie Holiday slaps Joel.

Alex belts him in the face and throws him through the doorway.

Alex puts his arms around Billie Holiday affectionately.

>   ALEX
>   Are you OK?

>   BILLIE HOLIDAY
>   You were fantastic. I saw your
>   performance. Promise me you'll see
>   mine.

>   ALEX
>   I promise.

INT. HOTEL - CLUB - NIGHT

A MASTER OF CEREMONIES assumes CENTER STAGE and stands in front
of a microphone.

>   MASTER OF CEREMONIES
>   Ladies and Gentleman. Miss Billie
>   Holiday!

Billie Holiday and her orchestra take the stage.

She SINGS as if each person was listening to his or her own
angel.

At the

BACK OF THE CLUB

Alex and the Lindy Hoppers try to enter, but MARTIN, the maitre
de, stops them.

>   MARTIN
>   Where do you think you're going, boy?
>   No Negroes allowed in the club.

>   ALEX
>   We're not Negroes--
>   (looks at name badge)
>   Martin. We're Lindy Hoppers from the
>   show.

>   MARTIN
>   I'll teach you to talk back, boy.

Martin tries to strike Alex, but Alex knocks him down.

SECURITY GUARDS

drag Alex and the rest of Lenny's Lindy Hoppers out of the club.

INT. BILLIE HOLIDAY'S DRESSING ROOM - NIGHT

Billie Holiday sits in a chair cleaning off her makeup.

KNOCKS sound off from her door.

>   WILLY
>   Come in.

Alex enters.

Stands next to her with an ICE-PACK on his head.

>   BILLIE HOLIDAY
>   What happened to you? Why didn't I see
>   any of you watching me sing.

>   ALEX
>   We tried, but they wouldn't let Colored
>   people in the club. I knew it happened
>   in the Jim Crow South, but this is
>   Boston.

>   BILLIE HOLIDAY
>   They did what!

Billie Holiday storms out of her dressing room.

INT. HOTEL OFFICE - NIGHT

Billie Holiday stands before MR. WAYNEWRIGHT, a pompous 55-
year-old Caucasian man, manager of the hotel.

>   MR. WAYNEWRIGHT
>   I'm very sorry Miss Holiday, but the
>   Hotel has a very strict policy: there
>   are no Negroes allowed in the club.

>   BILLIE HOLIDAY
>   Then, I guess it includes me, Mr.
>   Waynewright. We'll leave immediately.

Swingout

                    MR. WAYNEWRIGHT
          No, Miss Holiday, it does not apply to
          you.

                    BILLIE HOLIDAY
          You mean I can be on the stage but not
          looking at it. I don't perform
          anywhere where my people can't
          patronize.

                    MR. WAYNEWRIGHT
          You have no choice. We have a
          contract. We'll sue you.

                    BILLIE HOLIDAY
          Then sue.

                    MR. WAYNEWRIGHT
          The Governor is attending tomorrow
          night's performance. You can't do this
          to me.

INT. HOTEL - CLUB - NEXT NIGHT

A very upset crowd wonders why Billie Holiday has yet to take
the stage.

THREE SERCRET SERVICE TYPES approach a nervous MR. WAYNEWRIHGHT
in the back of the club.

                    SERCRET SERVICEMAN
          The Governor is a very busy man. Is
          there a problem?

INT. HOTEL — CLUB - NIGHT - LATER

The Lindy Hoppers all sit at a big table in the back of the
club with SMILES on their faces listening to BILLIE HOLIDAY
SING ON STAGE.

                    ALEX
          They could have at least given us a
          table in the middle. I can barely see.
          Why is Billie sitting on the floor?
          Oops. It's the drum set.

                    FREDA
          Alex, stop it. You're lucky we're even
          in here. If it was that easy to break
          the color line it would happen all the
          time.

                    ALEX
        There's no color line at The Savoy.

                    FREDA
        This ain't The Savoy.

                    MARGARET
        Billie Holiday sure is something else.

                    ALEX
        And so is Boston.

EXT. SAVOY BALLROOM — NIGHT

MARQUEE

"CAB CALLOWAY AND ERSKINE HAWKINS."

INT. SAVOY BALLROOM - NIGHT

ERSKINE HAWKINGS FINISHES PLAYING ON THE 140TH STREET STAGE.

CAB CALLOWAY performs on the 141ST STREET STAGE.

CAT'S CORNER

Alex, Freda, Willy, Margaret, James, Eydie, Bubba, and Ida are
all Swinging out.

                    FREDA
        Don't you think we should be practicing
        a routine for the second round of the
        Harvest Moon Swingout?

                    ALEX
        Practice. Please. Practicing is for
        amateurs. It'll be a piece of cake.

CURTIS'S BOOTH

Goody and Curtis sip on drinks.

                    CURTIS
        How was Boston?

                    GOODY
          How wasn't it? Not to mention almost
          getting beat down by security. While I
          was out on a fools errand, the kids
          decided to do Alex's routine instead of
          mine after Lenny expressively forbade
          them not to.

                    CURTIS
          How was it?

Goody doesn't answer.

                    CURTIS
          It won't be long before it'll be
          "Alex's" Lindy Hoppers. But, it's OK.
          You were ready to retire anyway,
          weren't you?

Goody looks out into

CAT'S CORNER

at Alex and Freda dancing and giggling.

EXT. SAVOY BALLROOM — DAY

Goody walks into the Savoy.

INT. SAVOY BALLROOM — OFFICE - DAY

Lenny speaks into the telephone with excitement.

                    LENNY
          March 5th, 6th, and 7th? I'm sorry I'm
          booked all month. Can you postpone the
          event? Maybe next time.

Goody mopes into the office.

                    LENNY
          Watch out there guy.

                    GOODY
          I don't want to be a stoolie.

                    LENNY
          Then don't. Alex and the kids did
          Alex's routine.

                    GOODY
          You knew? Why haven't you said
          anything?

                    LENNY
          I knew the night it happened.

Lenny tosses Goody a pile of MESSAGES.

                    LENNY
          Ever since it happened, the phone has
          been ringing off of the hook for Lindy
          Hoppers to come do that same routine.

                    GOODY
          I didn't know.

                    LENNY
          Alex is the future. He just needs some
          guidance. And with him on my team, I'm
          going to be the King of Swing.

INT. GERALDINE'S APARTMENT - NIGHT

Geraldine and Alex soak in a

HOT TUB

sipping from CHAMPAGNE glasses.

Geraldine

dips STRAWBERRIES into a bowl of WHIP CREAM and affectionately
feeds them to Alex as if he were a King.

                    GERALDINE
          I set up a date with you to meet Mary.

                    ALEX
          Who's Mary?

                    GERALDINE
          Your new partner.

                    ALEX
          I thought I already told you I have a
          partner.

                    GERALDINE
        You're too big for Lenny's little Lindy
        Hoppers. You need your own team. I
        could finance it.

                    ALEX
        I--

Geraldine plucks a strawberry into Alex's MOUTH.

                    GERALDINE
        Think about it first, all right? You
        know I'm right.

Alex sips from his glass of CHAMPAGNE.

EXT. ALEX'S APARTMENT BUILDING — DAY

Alex enters the building.

INT. ALEX'S APARTMENT - DAY

MOTHER WASHINGTON

lies cold and motionless in the living room floor.

ALEX

walks into the apartment and sees MOTHER WASHINGTON lying on
the floor.

He rushes over to her without closing the door.

                    ALEX
        Mama!

Alex checks her vital signs.

                          ALEX
                Help! Somebody help me!

EXT. HOSPITAL — DAY

An ambulance RINGING A SIREN speeds into the emergency
entrance.

INT. HOSPITAL ROOM - DAY

MOTHER WASHINGTON lies unconscious in a bed of a Pauper's Ward
with tubes hanging out of her arm.

Alex

kneels next to her with his HEAD on her womb.

A 59-YEAR-OLD DOCTOR

walks over to Alex and puts his hand on his shoulder.

                          DOCTOR
                It's time to go, son. Your mother
                needs her rest.

Alex pushes the Doctor's hands off of him.

TWO ORDERLIES

see and motion to assist.

THE DOCTOR

motions for them to wait.

                          DOCTOR
                The best thing you can do for your
                mother right now is be strong. Let her
                rest so you can come back and spend all
                your time with her when she has her
                strength.

ALEX

gets up and mashes his finger into the doctor's chest.

                          ALEX
                She'd better live or I'm holding you
                personally responsible.

Swingout

ALEX

walks away and kicks a BED PAN as he storms out of the ward.

EXT. SAVOY BALLROOM — DAY

Lenny enters the Savoy.

INT. SAVOY BALLROOM - DAY

The SAVOY SULTANS finish playing on stage.

Alex and Freda rehearse on the ballroom floor.

Freda breaks away and falls backwards on her ass.

                    ALEX
          Just follow me.

                    FREDA
          I'll never be able to follow you if I
          never know what you're trying to do.

Freda grabs Alex's hand.

They dance very aggressive with each other.

Freda intentionally TRIPS Alex.

He falls and bursts his LIP.

Freda laughs.

                    FREDA
          That's what you deserve. How does it
          feel?

                    ALEX
          You just don't get it do you?

Alex

gets up and walks away from her.

INT. SAVOY - LOBBY - DAY

Alex walks into the Lobby.

Bumps into Lenny.

> LENNY
> Leaving so soon? Where's Freda?

> ALEX
> I can't Lindy Hop with that beast.

Lenny

grabs Alex by the arm and leads him back towards the ballroom.

> LENNY
> I've let this go on far too long.

INT. SAVOY - BALLROOM - DAY

Lenny leads Alex into the Ballroom from out of the SHADOWS.

> LENNY
> Freda.

Freda throws a GLASS at Alex and it SHATTERS on the doorway.

> LENNY
> Damnit, girl. You almost hit me.

> FREDA
> I'm sorry, I didn't see you, Lenny.

> ALEX / FREDA
> I can't take it anymore--

> LENNY
> Hey! Quiet.

> LENNY
> (to Freda)
> I know your Mama raised you better than
> this. You've got to follow the leader.

> FREDA
> But--

                    LENNY
          Hush. And Alex, just because it's in
          your head doesn't mean the lady can
          follow it.

                    ALEX
          You don't understand--

                    LENNY
                 (cross)
          You don't know <u>what</u> I understand.

Lenny removes a handkerchief from his pocket and ties it over
his eyes.

                    LENNY
          I'm going to show you how it's done.

Alex and Freda are confused.

Lenny extends his hand to Freda.

                    FREDA
          I'm not dancing with you with a damn
          blindfold on.

                    FREDA
          Follow.

Freda grabs Lenny's hand defiantly.

They start dancing.

                    FREDA
          Not bad.

LENNY

leads Freda into a series of improvisational steps.

FREDA

follows all of them flawlessly.

                    FREDA
          Whooped by a blindfolded man. Hot
          damn.

Lenny extends his hand.

ALEX

leads Lenny onto the floor.

He Lindy Hops with him.

Lenny follows flawlessly.

>   LENNY
>   Too easy.

Alex does his best to throw Lenny off, but Lenny's follow remains flawless.

Freda claps.

>   FREDA
>   Why don't you two sweeties just dance
>   with each other for now on?

Lenny stops and removes the blindfold.

>   ALEX
>   How come you never told us you were
>   such a great Lindy Hopper? Why don't
>   you do that in a show with the team?

>   LENNY
>   I'm too old. I'd get in a show and try
>   to do something I couldn't execute and
>   probably kill myself.

LENNY

walks into the SHADOWS and out of the ballroom.

INT. SAVOY BALLROOM - DAY

Alex leads Freda onto the

DANCE FLOOR

>   ALEX
>   Let's try it again.

Alex and Freda Lindy Hop.

Alex and Freda Swingout with a strange lead.

She falls.

Swingout

                         FREDA
              What in the hell was that?

                         ALEX
              Just shut up and dance.

                         FREDA
              Don't talk to me like that. I'm not
              your child.

                         ALEX
              The only reason I'm still rehearsing is
              because you can't get it. I already
              know it all. It's here.

ALEX

points to his heart.

Turns his back to Freda.

FREDA,

FLAILING FISTS, screaming, charges Alex.

Hits him from behind with her shoulder knocking him down into a
TABLE.

Table breaks.

Freda beats on his FACE.

ALEX

tosses Freda off of him.

Manages to get up.

Tries to run, but Freda snatches his leg and pulls him onto the
FLOOR with her.

Breaks free.

FREDA

stands and charges Alex.

ALEX

SLAMS Freda onto the ground throwing his own body on top of
hers.

ALEX AND FREDA'S

LIPS attack each other like wild animals as they claw and
scrape away each other's garments.

INT. ALEX'S APARMENT — NIGHT

ALEX AND FREDA engage in the sexual equivalent of an ULTIMATE
FIGHTING CHAMPIONSHIP, tumbling throughout the apartment until
they plummet into terrifying ear curdling shrieks of CLIMAX.

EXT. HOSPITAL — DAY

Alex walks into the building.

INT. HOSPITAL - DAY

MOTHER WASHINGTON still lies unconscious with tubes hanging out
of her arm.

ALEX

kneels next to her and KISSES her on the cheek.

EXT. MEN'S CLOTHING STORE - DAY

Alex and Geraldine walk into the store with arms full of
shopping bags.

INT. MEN'S CLOTHING STORE - DAY

Alex walks out of a fitting room modeling a new pair of slacks.

                    ALEX
          What do you think?

                    GERALDINE
          I think you need to get rid of Freda
          tonight.

                    ALEX
          I'm tired about hearing this.

                    GERALDINE
          And I'm tired about being lied to.

GERALDINE

grabs Alex and rubs her LIPS sensually across his ear.

>   GERALDINE
>   (whispers)
>   If I find out you're fucking Freda, you
>   won't be fucking me or my money.

GERALDINE

slowly removes her lips from Alex's ear.

A SALESPERSON

gives Geraldine a STRANGE LOOK.

>   GERALDINE
>   I'll take that pair of slacks.

EXT. SAVOY BALLROOM — NIGHT

MARQUEE

"DINAH WASHINGTON & THE SAVOY SULTANS."

INT. SAVOY BALLROOM - NIGHT

THE SAVOY SULTANS finish playing on the 140TH STREET STAGE.

DINAH WASHINGTON sings on the 141ST STREET STAGE.

CAT'S CORNER

Alex & Freda, Willy & Margaret, James & Eydie, and Bubba & Ida
Swingout while LENNY walks amongst them like a coach.

>   ALEX
>   Let's take a break. We need to talk.

Freda follows Alex off of the dance floor.

They take a seat in a booth near CURTIS'S BOOTH where he is
sitting with Big Mabel, Richard, and Little Sally.

>   ALEX
>   It's about the other night.

>   FREDA
>   You think we should be dating.

>   ALEX
> I really like you, but I think we
> should just be partners, and not
> lovers.

Freda turns the TABLE upside down onto Alex.

This catches CURTIS'S attention.

>   FREDA
> Dance with somebody else!

MARGARET

runs over to Freda.

FREDA

puts her head in her hands and cries.

MARGARET

walks Freda away from Alex.

WILLY AND LENNY

run over to Alex.

>   WILLY
> Are you all right?

>   LENNY
> What's going on?

CURTIS

clinches his fist.

                    CURTIS (V.O.) (CONT'D)
          Victory!

EXT. SAVOY BALLROOM — NIGHT

MARQUEE

"BENNY GOODMAN & COUNT BASIE.   SECOND ROUND FOR THE HARVEST
MOON SWINGOUT."

INT. SAVOY BALLROOM - NIGHT

THE BENNY GOODMAN SEXTET plays on the 141ST STAGE.

WILLY AND MARGARET

Lindy Hop on the dance floor by themselves in the contest.

All of the contestants who have and have not danced are huddled
together in the

CAT'S CORNER

They include Alex & MARY WILLIS, Freda & Goody James & Eydie,
Curtis & Big Mabel, Richard & Little Sally, and PETE HARPER &
LISA SCANLON (a young Caucasian couple).

LENNY

is amongst them supporting his Lindy Hoppers.

WILLY AND MARGARET

finish their routine and join the other Lindy Hoppers.

                    MR. BUCHANAN
          Our next couple is Pete Harper and Lisa
          Scanlon.

PETE AND LISA

Swingout onto the dance floor.

                    ALEX
          How did a White couple qualify in round
          one?

>   EYDIE
>   They're from Jersey. I think they
>   qualified the night everybody took a
>   trip up to the Roseland.

Their Swingout is not as flashy as Alex's, but it's smooth and clean.

>   JAMES
>   Not bad, they work well together as a
>   team.

>   WILLY
>   For ballroom dancing.

James and Willy snicker.

The crowd gets behind Pete and Lisa.

They complete their routine and leave the dance floor.

>   WILLY
>   Nice job.

>   PETE / LISA
>   Thanks.

>   MR. BUCHANAN
>   The next couple is Alex & Mary.

>   ALEX
>   A one, a two, you know what to do.

>   MARY
>   Huh?

ALEX AND MARY

Swingout onto the dance floor.

Mary is unable to follow one of Alex's improvisational moves, but the crowd still supports them.

>   MARY
>   I'm sorry, try again.

Alex tries to execute more of his unique styling, but Mary is not able to follow.

They leave the dance floor.

Swingout

>   MR. BUCHANAN
>   Our last couple is Goody & Freda.

GOODY AND FREDA

Swingout onto the floor.

Their routine is plain, but pleasing.

>   FREDA
>   Shouldn't we do an airstep or
>   something?

>   GOODY
>   You should recognize I've been around
>   for awhile. It's wiser to play it
>   safe.

GOODY AND FREDA

look fine, but Goody is not able showoff Freda and maximize all
of her assets.

Goody and Freda complete their routine and leave the dance
floor.

>   MR. BUCHANAN
>   The judges have made their decision.
>   The four couples who will advance to
>   the final round of the Harvest Moon
>   Swingout are: Curtis & Big Mabel,
>   Richard & Little Sally, Willy &
>   Margaret...and it looks like we have a
>   tie for the fourth slot between Alex &
>   Mary and Goody & Freda.

>   WILLY
>   Sounds like I got a free dinner at
>   Small's, Alex.

>   MR. BUCHANAN
>   We're going to have to let the audience
>   decide, by round of applause.

CURTIS

dances in place with a huge SMILE on his face.

ALEX

fidgets in place with a look of DISGUST on his face.

                        MR. BUCHANAN
                Will it be Goody and Freda?

GOODY AND FREDA

casually walk into the dance floor.

They are greeted with warm applause.

                        FREDA
                Do something?

                        GOODY
                Why?

FREDA

grabs onto Goody's waist lowering herself into a split.

The crowd loves it.

                        MR. BUCHANAN (CONT'D)
                Or Alex and Mary?

ALEX AND MARY

walk into the dance floor.

They are greeted with equal applause.

                        ALEX
                Shit.

                        MR. BUCHANAN
                Goody and Freda?

                        ALEX
                Grab my hand.

                        MR. BUCHANAN (CONT'D)
                Or Alex and Mary?

ALEX

tries to execute a lift, but Mary can't carry her weight.

He drops her.

The crowd is silent for a beat.

                        MR. BUCHANAN
                Goody & Freda have it.

Swingout

                              FREDA
                         (to Alex)
              Yes! You lose.

ALEX

takes off his DANCING SHOES and hands them to LENNY.

                              ALEX
              I retire.

Walks away.

CURTIS

crouches on his knees with his arms stretched out to the
heavens.

                         CURTIS (V.O.)
              Thank you Jesus! I had fought the good
              fight of faith and my prayers had been
              answered. Alex Washington had lost and
              I was once again going to be crowned
              the King of Swing. Hallelujah!

INT. HOSPITAL — DAY

Alex sits in a chair holding Mother Washington's HAND while she
lies unconscious in bed.

                              ALEX
              You were right all along, Mama. I quit
              dancing. Tomorrow I'm going down to
              the Post Office to see if Mr.
              Fitzgerald can still give me a job.

Mother Washington's HAND squeezes Alex's hand tightly.

A hint of a SMILE forms on her face.

                        ALEX
          Doctor!

EXT. SAVOY BALLROOM — DAY

Curtis walks into the Savoy.

INT. SAVOY BALLROOM - DAY

THE CHICK WEBB ORCHESTRA rehearses on stage.

Goody & Freda, Willy & Margaret, Bubba & Ida, and James & Eydie
practice a new routine.

LENNY

sits in a chair observing.

                    LENNY
          Something is missing.

                    FREDA
          Let's throw in an airstep.

                    GOODY
          This is a dance team, not a circus.

Freda grabs Goody's hand.

                    FREDA
          Try this. Alex and I did this once at
          the Renaissance.

Goody tries to do a lift with Freda, but...

                    GOODY
          Ow, my back!

Goody drops Freda and collapses onto the floor.

EXT. POST OFFICE — DAY

Lenny walks into the Post Office.

INT. POST OFFICE - DAY

Lenny stands at the front counter talking to the Post Office
Manager, JAMES JOHSNON, an older African-American about Lenny's
age.

> LENNY
> Haven't seen you down at the Savoy
> lately, James. Thought you might like
> a couple of VIP passes so you won't
> have to wait in that crazy line.

> JAMES
> Thanks, Lenny. My old lady has been
> bugging me to go dancing. These are
> right on time.

> LENNY
> You mind if I talk to Alex for a
> moment?

EXT. GARMENT FACTORY - DAY

Lenny lights a CIGAR.

Freda sits on a stoop.

EXT. POST OFFICE - DAY

Alex and Lenny stand outside.

Lenny smokes a CIGAR.

> UNCHRONICLOGICAL INTERCUT TO:

LENNY & FREDA AND LENNY & ALEX

                    LENNY
          Are they treating you all right down
          here?

                    ALEX / FREDA
          It's a stable gig.

                    LENNY
          This is so hard for me to do, but I
          need your help.

Puffs on CIGAR.

                    LENNY (CONT'D)
          Dizzy Gillespie is playing at the
          Apollo and I promised him a couple
          Lindy Hoppers. Goody is in traction and
          everybody else on the team is already
          booked on gigs I promised months ago.
          Dizzy wasn't supposed to be here till
          next month, but he's here now.

Blows SMOKE.

                    LENNY (CONT'D)
          I know you are retired and don't dance
          with your old partner anymore. I
          wouldn't ask you to do it now that you
          have a career. I've always thought of
          you as my offspring and I need you to
          help your Dad out on this one. If
          anything else comes up, I'm telling
          them no until I get more Lindy Hoppers.

                    ALEX / FREDA
          I'll do it just this one time. And
          it's for you, not for you know who.

                    LENNY
          I knew I could count on you. Oh, you
          might need these.

Lenny gives Alex back his DANCING SHOES.

END UNCHRONILOGICAL INTERCUT SEQUENCE

EXT. APOLLO THEATRE — NIGHT

MARQUEE

"DIZZIE GILLESPIE."

INT. APOLLO THEATRE - NIGHT

Alex and Freda wait backstage.

They avoid talking and looking at each other, but eventually
break the ice.

                    FREDA
          Job?

                    FREDA
          Fine. Yours?

                    ALEX
          Fine. Mom?

                    FREDA
          Better. Yours?

                    ALEX
          Fine.

Silence.

The STAGE MANAGER approaches them.

                    STAGE MANAGER
          Lenny's Lindy Hoppers, you're on.

Alex and Freda mope onto

STAGE

ALEX AND FREDA

Swingout.

                    ALEX
          Want to do an Over-The-Back?

                        FREDA
              Just lead it.

The audience cheers.

                        FREDA
              Wanna' Freestyle.

                        ALEX
              Whatever, I'm with you.

ALEX AND FREDA

Freestyle.

The crowds screams.

Alex and Freda get into it.

ALEX

stops dancing completely.

Kneels before

FREDA

She solos.

The audience eats it up.

They start grooving.

Complete their routine.

Run

BACKSTAGE

elated, giggling arm in arm.

EXT. APPOLLO THEATRE - NIGHT

Alex and Freda stand on the sidewalk amidst a thick cloud of
FOG.

                        ALEX
              Did you hear them when I went on my
              knee and let you solo?

                    FREDA
          It was nothing. What about the flip we
          did from a Reverse Swingout?

ALEX

holds Freda in his arms.

                    ALEX / FREDA
          That one would be good in the Harvest
          Moon...

A beat.

                    FREDA
          I gotta' go. I need to get up in the
          morning.

                    ALEX
          Me too.

FREDA

runs away from Alex disappearing into the FOG.

INT. APOLLO THEATRE - DAY

Curtis sits in the office talking to the Apollo Owner, MR.
HOFFMAN, a 47-year-old Caucasian male who speaks by friendship,
but lives by money.

                    MR. HOFFMAN
          I'm sorry, Curtis. I know we go way
          back, but I have a contract with Lenny,
          now.

                    CURTIS
          Mr. Hoffman, my team hasn't had a gig
          in months.

                    MR. HOFFMAN
          I wish there was something I could do.
          Good luck to you.

                              CURTIS (V.O.)
                    How could everybody in town have a
                    contract with Lenny? Lenny was
                    muscling me out and it was because of
                    boy wonder, Alex Washington. I should
                    have killed him when I had the chance.

EXT. SAVOY BALLROOM — DAY

Freda walks into the Savoy with LEFTY WALKER, a short, comical
young African-American male in his early 20's.

INT. SAVOY BALLROOM — OFFICE - DAY

Freda and Lefty are seated before Mr. Buchanan who is behind
his desk.

                              MR. BUCHANAN
                    I'm sorry, Freda. I have nothing
                    against Lefty, but these are the same
                    rules we've had since the first Harvest
                    Moon Swingout. During the third round
                    of competition, a partner may not dance
                    with anyone who has not qualified in
                    any of the previous rounds.

EXT. SAVOY BALLROOM — NIGHT

MARQUEE

"FATS WALLER & MARTIN RUSHING."

Alex walks into the Savoy.

INT. SAVOY BALLROOM - NIGHT

FATS WALLER finishes playing on the 140TH STREET STAGE.

MARTIN RUSHING PLAYS on the 141ST STREET STAGE.

CAT'S CORNER

Freda sits at a booth with Willy, Margaret, Bubba, and Ida.

ALEX

approaches Freda.

Swingout

                    WILLY
Long time no see, stranger.

                    BUBBA
I heard you and Freda brought the house
down at the Apollo. How much did they
pay you?

                    MARGARET
Ask her to dance.

                    ALEX
Can I speak first? Freda, would you
Lindy with me, please?

                    FREDA
Not if you're only asking because
everybody wants you to.

                    ALEX
You're impossible.

Alex turns his back.

                    FREDA
No, wait. I'll dance, cry baby.

Alex leads Freda onto the

DANCE FLOOR

                    FREDA
I've been thinking, maybe we should
work together again.

                    ALEX
I thought we weren't partners anymore.

                    FREDA
We wouldn't be partners, but
partnering.

                    ALEX
Why?

                    FREDA
So, we can win the Harvest Moon
Swingout. I have to dance with someone
who has already qualified, which means-
—

>   ALEX
>   I'm the only candidate on the list.
>   So, you want to use me. Good night,
>   Freda. You're hopeless.

Alex turns his back.

>   FREDA
>   Alex!

Freda grabs Alex.

>   ALEX
>   What!

>   FREDA
>   Please be my partner again.

>   ALEX
>   No.

>   FREDA
>   I need you and you need me. Besides
>   you want to win the contest as much as
>   I do.

>   ALEX
>   Maybe.

>   FREDA
>   But, there's only one catch.

INT. SAVOY BALLROOM — OFFICE - DAY

Lenny sits at his desk dialing a telephone number.

Alex and Freda barge into his office.

>   FREDA
>   Teach us the secret of leading and
>   following.

INT. SAVOY - BALLROOM - DAY

Alex and Freda stand at the edge of the dance floor listening
to Lenny.

                    LENNY
          You and Freda have been working against
          each other all this time. You have to
          work with one another as one. One
          mind, one body, one spirit.

Lenny blindfolds Freda.

ALEX AND FREDA

Swingout onto the dance floor.

                    LENNY
          Alex, the man's job is to make the
          woman look good. You should always do
          whatever it takes for her to follow
          your lead. You don't try to out dance
          her, you try to make her out dance you.

FREDA

dances clumsily with Alex with the blindfold on.

                    LENNY
          Freda, it's the woman's job to follow
          the man. You have to concentrate to
          make your body an extension of his
          movement. You have no style except for
          the style of the man you are following.
          Always concentrate on how well you look
          together.

Lenny removes Freda's blindfold and puts it on Alex.

                    LENNY
          Your bodies must be one. There are no
          limits.

Lenny slides Alex's hands over Freda's derriere.

                    LENNY (CONT'D)
          When you're on the dance floor, Freda
          is the only woman in the world, and
          Alex is the only man in the world. You
          must make love on the dance floor.

Alex and Freda snicker.

                    LENNY
          Practicing is dating, dancing is making
          love, and airsteps are climaxes.

LENNY

puts another blindfold on Freda so neither Freda nor Alex can
see.

                    LENNY
          Dance is passionate. Without passion,
          it's just movement in space.

ALEX AND FREDA

are still timid with each other's bodies.

                    LENNY
          And the single most important thing
          is...

A beat.

                    ALEX / FREDA
          What?

                    LENNY
          Magic. You have to have magic. A
          couple with magic between the two of
          them is undefeatable. Master all of
          these principles, and you shall be the
          King and Queen of Swing.

LENNY

walks away from the dance floor and disappears into the
SHADOWS.

EXT. HOSPITAL — DAY

Alex sits next to Mother Washington lying in her hospital bed.
Tubes still hang from her arm, but she is coherent.

                    MOTHER WASHINGTON
          You seem happier today, how's the job.

                    ALEX
          It's a career.

A beat.

                    ALEX (CONT'D)
Freda and I danced at the Apollo for
Dizzy Gillespie. For the first time
ever, Freda and I were truly dancing as
one. It was like we could read each
other minds. We decided to get back
together to compete in the finals for
the Harvest Moon Swingout.

                    MOTHER WASHINGTON
Alex, I love you and I want good things
for you. A career at the Post Office
is a good thing, but so is happiness.
I want you to make me a promise.

                    ALEX
Anything, Mama.

                    MOTHER WASHINGTON
If you want to be a Swing dancer, be
the greatest Swing dancer who ever
lived. I want you and Freda to win the
Harvest Moon Swingout. Now, go
rehearse.

Alex kisses Mother Washington affectionately.

                    ALEX
I love you.

Alex runs out of the ward.

                    MOTHER WASHINGTON
And don't come back here until you have
a trophy.

EXT. GERALDINE'S APARTMENT BUILDING - NIGHT

Alex walks into the building carrying several shopping bags.

INT. GERALDINE'S APARTMENT - NIGHT

Geraldine experiences a tirade while Alex stands his ground.

                    GERALDINE
No. I expressly forbid it.

                    ALEX
It's not your decision to make. I came
here tonight to tell you we're history.

                    GERALDINE
          You can't do this. You need me.

                     ALEX
          No, I don't need you or your money. I
          came here tonight to give you back
          everything you bought me. As a matter
          of fact, I think you bought this shirt
          I'm wearing, too.

ALEX

takes the shirt off of his back and stuffs it into one of the
shopping bags.

GERALDINE

puts her arms around Alex and tries to KISS him.

                    GERALDINE
          You'll be back, because you want my
          money.

Alex pries Geraldine's hands off of him.

                     ALEX
          Correction. I'm not for sale. Denied.
          Account closed.

Alex walks out of the apartment.

Geraldine throws a LAMP at Alex.

The lamp CRASHES into a closing door.

                              DISSOLVE TO:

MONTAGE SEQUENCE — SEVERAL DAYS

INT. SAVOY BALLROOM — DAY

THE CHICK WEBB ORCHESTRA rehearses on stage.

Alex and Freda rehearse.

                     ALEX
          Let's try the move we did in the first
          round of the Harvest Moon.

> FREDA
> It was nice, but everybody has already
> seen it. If you really want to beat
> Curtis, we need to stick with the
> formula and come up with something new.

Alex and Freda experiment with new moves.

Some are sloppy, others are clean.

> FREDA
> The Jump and Flip you did in round two
> was kind of cool. I just wasn't
> prepared. Let's think up a variation
> on it.

Alex and Freda continue to experiment.

Alex drops Freda.

She laughs and shakes it off.

Alex falls.

He laughs and shakes it off as Freda helps him up.

> ALEX
> I've got it. What about a variation on
> Curtis's routine? It's like, oh, we've
> seen it before, then pow--out of
> nowhere we throw in a twist.

> FREDA
> I like that idea.

Alex and Freda try to work it out.

Freda twists her ANKLE.

Alex wraps it up with an ACE BANDAGE.

They continue to rehearse.

Alex twists his knee.

Freda wraps up his knee with an ACE BANDAGE.

Alex and Freda continue to Lindy Hop.

Alex and Freda sweat pervasively.

Their sweaty hands lose grip of each other and Alex Swings
Freda out flying across the dance floor.

> FREDA
> That's it!

> ALEX
> Freda, I'm sorry, our hands were so
> sweaty.

> FREDA
> No, the move. Dry off you hands. We
> can Swingout like that and both go into
> a Free Spin. Then I know what will
> definitely crown us the undisputed King
> and Queen of Swing.

> ALEX
> What is it?

Freda smiles.

> FREDA
> Can you keep a secret?

Alex and Freda continue to Lindy Hop.

They slowly start to catch on and explore each other's bodies
through dance.

Alex and Freda remove their blindfolds.

Alex executes a lift and Freda performs it flawlessly.

Alex pulls Freda's body close to his and their LIPS slowly meet
escalating into passionate foreplay.

END MONTAGE SEQUENCE

> DISSOLVE TO:

INT. ALEX'S APARTMENT — NIGHT

Alex's and Freda's bodies are entwined in intense, passionate
love-making.

They work together pleasing each other until they arrive at a harmonious magical climax.

EXT. SAVOY BALLROOM — NIGHT

MARQUEE

"JO STAFFORD & SARAH VAUGHN."

A 40-year-old PHOTOGRAPHER enters the Savoy.

INT. SAVOY BALLROOM - NIGHT

JO STAFFORD finishes playing on the 140TH STREET STAGE.

SARAH VAUHGN SINGS on the 141ST STREET STAGE.

CAT'S CORNER

Alex and Freda SHOWOFF in a

JAM CIRCLE

Alex pulls Freda tight to his body and kisses her while spinning there bodies as one unit.

As Alex launches Freda into an airstep, a PHOTOGRAPHER snaps a picture.

Alex and Freda leave the Jam Circle.

The photographer runs over to them.

                    PHOTOGRAPHER
          You kids are fantastic. I've been
          photographing dance for nearly twenty
          years and I've never seen anything as
          magical as what I just saw now.

Alex and Freda kiss.

                    PHOTOGRAPHER
          Can I ask you a few questions?

                          ALEX / FREDA
          Sure.

EXT. SAVOY BALLROOM — DAY

Curtis picks up LIFE MAGAZINE from a newsstand and beholds a

PICTURE

of Alex and Freda dancing in a feature layout.

Curtis rips the article out of the magazine and tosses in the
TRASH.

                          CURTIS (V.O.)
          Nooooooooooooooooooooooooooooo!   God was
          laughing at me.

The NEWSSTAND ATTENDANT detains Curtis.

                          NEWSSTAND ATTENDANT
          Hey, you gotta' pay for that.

EXT. SAVOY BALLROOM — NIGHT

Thousands of people are crowded around the Savoy.

MARQUEE

"HARVEST MOON SWINGOUT FINALS & THE CHICK WEBB ORCHESTRA."

INT. SAVOY BALLROOM - NIGHT

THE CHICK WEBB ORCHESTRA plays on the 140ST STREET STAGE.

Alex & Freda, Willy & Margaret, Curtis & Big Mabel, and Richard
and Little Sally all wait backstage.

Mr. Buchanan comes backstage holding a HAT filled with four
small folded pieces of paper.

                          MR. BUCHANAN
          We're ready to start the lottery.

MS. CLARKE rushes backstage.

                         MS. CLARKE
              Alex, Mother Washington has gotten
              worse. They don't think she's going to
              make it. You've got to go to the
              hospital.

                         FREDA
              Don't worry about the contest.

Alex hesitates.

                         ALEX
              If she's all right I'll come back.
              It's only 10 blocks from here.

                         FREDA
              Go!.

Alex runs out of the BACK DOOR.

                         MR. BUCHANAN
              Would each lady please pick a number
              from the hat?

LITTLE SALLY

grabs a piece of paper from the hat.

She opens it up and shows it to Richard.

                         RICHARD
              No! First position.   The kiss of
              death. We've lost.

                         LITTLE SALLY
              Shut up, fool.

                         RICHARD
              You know the first two couples always
              lose.

BIG MABEL

takes a piece of paper from the hat and shows it to Curtis.

                         CURTIS
              Number three. Good spot.

FREDA

selects a piece of paper from the hat.

                        FREDA
          Last.

EXT. RAILROAD CROSSING - NIGHT

A TRAIN WHISTLE blows.

In the distance, ARMS FOLD DOWN over the railroad tracks for an
incoming TRAIN.

ALEX

tries to run through the gate, but the

TRAIN

is too close.

ALEX

waits with frustration.

INT. SAVOY BALLROOM - NIGHT

All of the contestants enter from backstage and wait in the

CAT'S CORNER

Mr. Buchanan walks onto the center of 141ST STREET STAGE and
over to a microphone.

                    MR. BUCHANAN
          Ladies and gentlemen, tonight our four
          finalist couples will compete for
          $5,000 cash in the 10th Annual Harvest
          Moon Swingout. Winners take all.

The crowd cheers.

                    MR. BUCHANAN (CONT'D)
          Our first couple is Richard & Little
          Sally.

RICHARD AND LITTLE SALLY

Swingout on to the dance floor.

RICHARD

wins the crowd over with his signature CRAZY LEGS.

EXT. RAILROAD CROSSING - NIGHT

The ARMS RISE above the railroad tracks.

ALEX

sprints across.

EXT. HOSPITAL - NIGHT

Alex dashes into the building.

INT. HOSPITAL - NIGHT

Alex races through the Pauper's Ward. A nurse holds Mother
Washington's hand.

                         NURSE
              She's been calling for you.

                         ALEX
              Mama, it's me. I'm here for you.

                    MOTHER WASHINGTON
              Did you win?

                         ALEX
              Forget the contest.

                    MOTHER WASHINGTON
              No, I want you to win.
                    (coughs)
              I can't see Jesus until I <u>know</u> my boy
              will be happy.

                         ALEX
              Nothing is more important to me than my
              mother.

                    MOTHER WASHINGTON
              And nothing is more important to me
              than my only son's happiness.

Weakly forms a FIST and hits Alex.

                    MOTHER WASHINGTON
          Go.
                    (coughs)
          Go.

                         NURSE
          You better go. You're upsetting her.

                    MOTHER WASHINGTON
          Bring your Mama the trophy.

                         ALEX
          I will. I promise.

Alex runs out of the Pauper's Ward.

INT. SAVOY BALLROOM - NIGHT

Richard and Little Sally leave the dance floor.

Freda stares at her

WATCH HANDS

"11:33 P.M."

                         RICHARD
          Our best performance, yet. We had a
          really unique Swingout. Why couldn't
          we have gone last?

                       LITTLE SALLY
          Somebody had to go first.

                       MR. BUCHANAN
          Our next couple is Willy & Margaret.

WILLY AND MARGARET

Swingout onto the dance floor.

Their routine is full of DEATH DEFYING tricks.

Willy and Margaret's bodies become drenched with SWEAT, but
they neither slip nor slide out of each other's grasp.

The crowd goes INSANE.

EXT. STREET - NIGHT

Alex's HEART POUNDS as he races in the middle of the street on
foot.

INT. SAVOY BALLROOM - NIGHT

Willy and Margaret leave the dance floor.

FREDA paces back and forth.

Stares at her

WATCH HANDS

"11:47 P.M."

> MR. BUCHANAN
> It's starting to get hot in here. Our
> next couple is our reigning
> champions...

The house LIGHTS DIM.

THE CHICK WEBB ORCHESTRA plays KINGLY MUSIC.

> MR. BUCHANAN (CONT'D)
> For nine consecutive years, the
> undefeated King of Queen of Swing
> Shooooooooooooooooooooorty Moore!

The house LIGHTS RAISE.

CURTIS

walks into the dance floor by himself wearing a CROWN and a
KING'S ROBE.

His hands are stretched high above his head in "V" formation
VICTORY STANCE.

A large SCEPTRE is clasp in a hand.

> FREDA
> I think I'm going to throw up.

> MR. BUCHANAN
> And Biiiiiiiiiiiiiiiiiiiiiig Mabel!

Curtis BOWS on one knee.

THREE BUFF MUSCLEHEADS

oiled and draped in loincloths, carry

Big Mabel

stretched out above their heads.

Big Mabel is adorned in a matching CROWN and ROBE.

>   WILLY
>   Now, you can throw up.

The Muscleheads place Big Mabel next to Curtis and take away
the CROWNS, ROBES, and SCEPTRE.

EXT. STREET - NIGHT

Alex is tripped by a MUGGER. He points a gun at Alex.

>   MUGGER
>   Don't move.

>   ALEX
>   You picked the wrong Negro on wrong
>   night.

ALEX

kicks the gun at of the MUGGER's hand and knocks him out cold
in one punch.

INT. SAVOY BALLROOM - NIGHT

APPLAUSE.

THE CHICK WEBB ORCHESTRA plays an awesome Swinging tune.

Curtis and Big Mabel

Swingout.

The crowd cheers for every move.

The routine is WONDROUS in its comedy as well as it's precision
and execution.

Curtis and Big Mabel climax their routine with their signature EXIT.

Big Mabel and Curtis stand back to back with arms locked.

Big Mabel bends forward carrying Curtis on her back.

MR. BUCHANAN

tries to talk into the microphone, but the crowd will not stop cheering.

CURTIS

giggles maniacally.

> CURTIS (V.O.)
> It was the performance of a lifetime.
> Big Mabel and I had never danced so
> well before, and never would again. I
> couldn't possibly lose. I knew I had
> won. I was still the King of Swing.
> Since it was my tenth victory, I was
> considering retiring.

EXT. SAVOY - ALLEY - NIGHT

Alex bursts through the door into the building.

INT. SAVOY BALLROOM - NIGHT

Mr. Buchanan waits at the microphone for the cheers to die down.

Freda stares at her

WATCH HANDS

"12:00 MINDNIGHT"

> CURTIS
> I guess it's over, so you can start
> singing, Big Mabel.

Several people slap CURTIS & BIG MABEL on the back congratulating them on their victory.

Alex

leaps over someone's head into the

CAT'S CORNER

The crowd screams.

He holds Freda close to him.

>   ALEX / FREDA
>   One mind, one body, one spirit.

>   ALEX
>   Let's make some magic.

>   MR. BUCHANAN
>   And our final couple in the 10th Annual
>   Harvest Moon Swingout is Alex
>   "Washington" Washington & Freda
>   Fitzgerald!

>   ALEX
>   A one--

>   FREDA
>   a two--

>   ALEX / FREDA
>   You know what to do.

ALEX AND FREDA

Swingout onto the dance floor.

ALEX AND FREDA

Lindy Hop with a passion they have never had before.

CHIC WEBB, 32-years-old, is captivated.

>   CHICK WEBB
>   I think the kids are really going for
>   it.

Alex and Freda are completely IN SYNC with the music.

CHICK WEBB

catches every lift, drop, and spin with snare rolls, cymbal
crashes, and bass drum thumps.

CURTIS

gets uncomfortable.

Swingout

ALEX AND FREDA

break into an intricate freestyling routine.

                    WILLY
          You go boy!

                    MARGARET
          You go girl.

AS ALEX AND FREDA SWINGOUT,

they slide out of each others hands.

Put on

BLINDFOLDS

Spin back into each other.

                    LENNY
          Magic.

ALEX AND FREDA

continue dancing by doing VARIATIONS on Curtis's routine.

The CHEERS of the crowd start to drown out the sound of the
music.

ALEX AND FREDA

climax the routine by initiating an airstep, still in
blindfolds, where Freda rolls over Alex's back and onto the
floor in sync with the end of the music.

The crowd is dead SILENT for a beat.

Suddenly everyone erupts into THUNDEROUS ear piercing applause.

The entire crowd runs onto the dance floor and picks

ALEX AND FREDA

up on their hands carrying them through the

CAT'S CORNER

                    MR. BUCHANAN
          I guess the kids won it.

KIP TURNER

pushes his way through the crowd.

> KIP TURNER
> I'm choreographing a Lindy Hop scene
> for the movie version of "Jive
> Talkin'". I saw you in Boston and I
> want you all to do the same routine in
> the movie.

> ALEX
> Hollywood, here we come.

Curtis

puts his head down between his legs.

BIG MABEL

comforts him.

As people run past Curtis to get to Alex and Freda, someone
accidentally steps on his ROBE, tearing it, while someone else
kicks his CROWN.

> MR. BUCHANAN
> Alex, where did you get that routine
> from?

CURTIS AND BIG MABEL

stare at Alex.

> ALEX
> From Curtis and Lenny. Lenny taught us
> how to Lindy Hop with blindfolds and
> the last airstep was just a variation
> on Curtis and Big Mabel's exit.

A single TEAR rolls down

CURTIS'S FACE

while a hint of a smile forms.

                              CURTIS (V.O.)
                    I had become so self-absorbed with
                    winning, I thought of Alex as my enemy,
                    not realizing Alex thought of himself
                    as an extension of me. I had the named
                    of the Lindy Hop, but Alex was it's
                    evolution.

EXT. HOSPITAL — NIGHT

Alex and Freda RUN into the hospital carrying trophies.

INT. HOSPITAL - NIGHT

Alex tries to enter the Paupers Ward, but is stopped by an
ORDERLY.

                              ORDERLY
                    I'm sorry sir, you can't go in there.
                    Visiting hours are over.

ALEX

PUSHES the orderly onto the ground and grabs Freda's hand.

They sprint into the

PAUPER'S WARD

MOTHER WASHINGTON

lies in bed barely conscious.

                              ALEX
                    Mama, we won.

ALEX

shows Mother Washington the TROPHIES.

FREDA

clears her throat.

                              ALEX
                    Oh, and this is Freda.

                              MOTHER WASHINGTON
                    So, nice to finally meet you. I see
                    why he's so crazy about you.

                         FREDA
          I'm crazy about him, too.

                    MOTHER WASHINGTON
          I knew you could do it. Everything is
          going to be fine now. Trust me.

MOTHER WASHINGTON

lays her head on her pillow and closes her eyes.

Her heart stops beating.

                         ALEX
               Mama?

ALEX

checks her vital signs.

                    ALEX (CONT'D)
          Noooooooooooooooooooooooooooo!

TEARS stream down

ALEX'S FACE

as ORDERLIES and NURSES run over to the bed.

EXT. CEMETARY - DAY

ALEX

stands with Freda in front of the gravesite where Mother
Washington's CASKET lies.

ALL CAST MEMBERS FROM THE SAVOY

are in attendance at the funeral.

A 58-year-old preacher finishes a prayer.

                         PREACHER
          For thine is the kingdom, and the
          glory, and the power, forever, and
          ever, amen.

ALEX

lays his Harvest Moon

Swingout

TROPHY

on top of Mother Washington's CASKET.

                    ALEX
          Amen.

UNDERTAKERS

slowly lower the

CASKET

into the ground.

FREDA

puts her arm around Alex and kisses him on the cheek.

ALEX AND FREDA

walk away together into the SUNSET.

FADE OUT.

                    THE END